30 Days
to Me

30 Days to Me

Lynn Reilly

Sacred Stories
PUBLISHING

30 Days to Me
Lynn Reilly
Tradepaper ISBN: 978-1-945026-40-9
Electronic ISBN: 978-1-945026-41-6

Library of Congress Control Number: 2017956633

Published by Sacred Stories Publishing
https://sacredstoriespublishing.com

Printed in the United States of America

Dedication

To You- for choosing to live your life as it's meant to be- Serendipitously.
As you allow more joy into your life, the rest of us are inspired to do the same,
and that's how we change the world.

Acknowledgments

With all the gratitude my heart can muster, I'd like to thank…

My children, Ella and Jackson, for listening to my endless stories and supporting me with unconditional love, respect, fantastic humor and all the inspiration a Mom could hope for.

My family for cheerleading me on and loving me for who I am, especially my father, John, and step mom, Mary Ann, for supporting me even when my decisions seemed scary, but trusting enough to stand by me no matter what.

My oldest and most trusted confidantes, Tara, Becca, and Jeannie for sticking with me as I changed my entire world and keeping me grounded… while reading countless writings and helping me sift through thousands of ideas with patience and open mindedness.

My feedback crew and amazing friends who came in at the exact time I needed you in my life, Julie, Ruth, and Tami. For helping me in insurmountable ways while writing this book…with laughter, editing, processing, processing and more processing…than friends should have to endure.

Sacred Stories Publishing for all the work that went into this book, editing, designing and especially the encouragement and patience to work with me while I wrote and rewrote what felt best.

My many, many clients and students who've taught me the meaning of true compassion, nonjudgment, and the understanding that we are all in this together.

My Inspirologist, Jayne, who continues to be my treasured friend, guide and editor in Spirit and all the gentle and not so gentle nudges to keep going.

And the game changer in my life, Erik. For inspiring me to turn myself inside out and discover the beautiful Me within. Forever grateful.

You. You're Missing You.

I sat on my front porch, sobbing; my heart felt completely broken into pieces. The pangs of loss were fierce. I felt the grief from the past few years flood me—a lifetime of emotion. It was a huge wave, overpowering, and devastatingly harsh. The pain felt all too familiar.

"Why is this happening to me?" I questioned. "What was I missing?"

And then I heard the little voice pipe in. You know the one. The one that always seems to know the answers.

"You. You're missing you. You've spent your life focusing on everyone else. It's time to focus on you."

My tears began to slow down. I wasn't sure what it meant, but I was intrigued. I asked for more answers, and they came.

"Learn how to love you. Reconnect with yourself. Love and accept who you are, and the rest will fall into place."

Hmm, sounds lovely, but really, I wasn't sure I knew how. I felt disconnected, lost, sad, lonely, angry, confused, and lots of other downer words that could fill up a page. But I knew there was some truth to those statements. And I wanted to learn how to do it.

I again asked that voice to speak up. "Tell me what to do!" I demanded.

I could have been a little gentler, but I was feeling impatient, and my nature is not one who appreciates waiting.

The inspiration came quickly. I knew exactly how to love and support others; that's what I did best. Now I had to learn how to love and support myself. And it had to be enjoyable. No more of this tortured stuff. I needed to treat myself as a priority, with the attention I was craving, and I was determined to do just that. I was to take the next thirty days to create a new habit—the habit of taking care of myself, my needs, my priorities—and try something new.

My pattern of putting others first began when I was a young child. My mother had her first "episode," as my father called them, when I was nine months old. "Episode" was defined as an emotional breakdown when she could no longer cope with the stressors of her life. My mother had bouts of delusion, disoriented states, debilitating depression, and highs interspersed between the lows. Her initial diagnosis was paranoid schizophrenia, and she later received a diagnosis of and treatment for manic depression.

My childhood was spent watching my mother ride the waves of excessive highs and deep and disturbing lows. She made various suicide attempts, and spent many dark days in her room trying to will herself out of her sorrow-filled emotional instability. Innately sensitive and an eager listener, I became her confidante. She referred to me as her "little psychiatrist," as I continuously attempted to help her work her way out of her profoundly depressed state.

According to my mother, I always knew what to say, and she wondered how. I told her that God spoke through me to help her. Otherwise, I had no answer. How could I? I was eight years old, maybe nine.

I recall skipping school a lot and pretending to be ill to stay home with my mother. I worried for her safety and well-being. She did not do well on her own, and I felt an ongoing sense of responsibility to help her.

As I grew toward adolescence and my parents separated and divorced, I began to grow weary of the need to take care of my mother. I wanted to be a normal kid with kid problems and adolescent drama, and I did my very best to make this happen.

I began to pull away from her as she continued to spiral downward. When she no longer lived with us, it was easier to keep my distance. It was also easier for her to drift further toward her demise. After several more episodes and cries for help, my mother took her life less than a week before my fifteenth birthday. My call to duty for her ended in heartbreak, but it would only begin my drive to help others in any way I could.

I was always the person people were drawn to talk with and share their concerns. I never understood why I felt responsible for other people's well-being or why I felt things so deeply; I just knew I did. If someone was in need, I felt compelled to be a part of their healing. I did not know as a child that I was an empath, someone who is sensitive to feel other people's feelings and often sense their thoughts.

It was no surprise that psychology would be the field I chose to study in college. I was thrilled to learn that talking and listening to people was an actual skill. My career in counseling allowed me to put other people first. It was my job, so it seemed necessary. However, my personal life followed the same pattern.

I made myself available to all of my friends, to be the one they could rely on. I would always stop what I was doing to listen, advise, and support. The hallmark of my romantic relationships was the same. I often was consumed with whether they were okay. And when/if they tried to support me, I found myself pulling away. *Didn't they see I had to carry the weight of the world on my own?*

When I married, the pattern continued. I wanted to be everything for my husband, and an independent person too. The codependent tendencies I helped create started to creep in. When I had children, the desire to be more than enough was fierce. Because of my childhood, I wasn't sure if I knew how to mother, so I put all of my energy, knowledge, and emotion into taking care of my kids. Not only did it seem important, but it also felt like the cultural norm. To be a "good" parent, one must put all of one's focus on the children. I bought into it. And due to my fears, I didn't want them ever to feel neglected or uncared for, so I was determined to find ways to shield them from these human realities. I was certain there must be a way.

Going back to work, I felt immense guilt for leaving my daughter during the day for so long. My anxiety level was through the roof with the amount of pressure I put on myself to be perfect at everything. For support, I went to a mental health counselor the year after my daughter was born, as I could not seem to stop worrying that I was not going to get it right.

I relaxed a bit when my son was born, and less than two years later my husband lost his job and stayed home with our kids. Having him home took some pressure off me to do and be it all for our children. But I still felt like I couldn't do or be enough. I felt guilt when I was not with them.

I remember the long days and nights of anxiety. I tried to distract myself from my discomfort and the feeling of being small and insignificant. I felt as if I was missing something.

I was unhappy, but I didn't know why. Something was changing inside me, and I couldn't escape it. There was nowhere for me to go. I wasn't even sure who I was underneath this skin of mine, but whoever I was becoming, she wanted to come out and be seen. And that scared me very much.

I felt disconnected from my husband and our life. We both were changing as we began to travel down different paths. I cannot recall the moment I realized I couldn't be married anymore. I know it was progressive, and I know it was heart-wrenching, but all I remember now is the aftermath. I was devastated for both of us, for our family. I wanted so badly to make it work, but I couldn't. My anguish was eating me up. It was time to let it go.

I will never forget the sheer panic I felt when I told my husband I couldn't see us together anymore. It was not at all what I thought I'd signed up for, what I'd planned.

The separation and divorce process was undoubtedly one of the most difficult and painful experiences of my life. Making the decision to let go had been challenging, but following through was even harder. Reality felt beastly, and I couldn't escape it.

I felt incredibly selfish, in a negative way, but I knew it was the best decision for all of us. And it was. It was the first of many decisions I would make for the next couple of years that, selfish or not, were the best choices I could have made, pain and all.

From leaving one career passion to follow another, to letting go of friends who pulled away and no longer supported me, to opening my heart when it wanted to close up, and to taking leaps of faith in various areas of my life, I knew I was onto something. I was feeling more alive and had greater clarity, but many of my long-standing patterns were still intact and continued to affect me.

As I sat there on my porch that day, crumbling, shaking, heart feeling shattered, I knew it was my wake-up call, my opportunity to try something new. To get to know me, my authentic self, the part that was begging to come out. She was ready.

And so *30 Days to Me* was born. I started by creating a list of things I enjoyed doing or things I wanted to learn or try. I committed to prioritizing myself every single day. No matter what was going on, I was building in some me time and adding in indulgences for myself everywhere I could. My goal was to treat myself with the same respect and generosity that I easily gifted to others. I would learn to take care of me. I would be self-aware.

I also decided to include a focus for each day to gain a better understanding of myself. I wanted to learn more about why I kept ending up in the same place emotionally. Journaling and introspection became a key component in discerning parts of myself that had not been discovered or had not had any light shined on them. The questions in this book come from listening to my inner voice with a desire to get to know myself at a deeper level. I learned to acknowledge my behavior and thought patterns, and to recognize if and where they needed to be tweaked.

I believe it is my purpose in life to teach and share what I have learned. I am grateful to have the opportunity to pass it on.

Have you ever hit a point in your life where you feel off, disconnected, and somewhat detached from what you enjoy and care about the most? Often these feelings creep up, and you realize you don't feel the same. Sometimes symptoms of depression, such as deteriorated mood, lethargy, and sad or angry thoughts make an unwelcomed appearance, letting you know that something is off. While other times, symptoms of anxiety such as edginess, irritability, pervasive fear, worrisome thoughts, muscle tension, and waves of panic can pop up. At this point, all you know is you don't feel good, and you're not sure how you got there or how to find your way out. You know you want to change, but often you don't know how.

Change is minimally a two-part process. Part one is gaining an understanding of yourself through self-awareness. The more you look inward at what you want and don't want, as well as how you respond, the more you understand why the same types of people and experiences keep entering your life. Part two is action, doing something different than you typically do. Self-awareness gives you knowledge of why you do what you do, but an action is what is required if you want anything to shift. You cannot have change without action, just as you do not know what to change without self-awareness. They go hand in hand.

This book, *30 Days to Me*, is designed to help you reconnect with your authentic self and recognize the love and support within and around you. As you dig deep, you will discover your thought and behavior patterns and have a greater sense of who you are. You will learn what it is you need to feel more balance and ease. You will also be guided to recognize the joy in your life that already exists, thus increasing your faith and understanding that the more you give to yourself, the more you will also receive.

Committing to this process for thirty days or longer can teach you valuable information, while giving yourself space and opportunity to treat yourself in the loving way you treat others.

When you feel depleted, you only have so much to give. Filling your cup gives you more to give to others. Taking care of yourself and being self-aware of your needs and fulfilling them is the most responsible and effective way you can help yourself stay healthy, strong, and with the capacity to give even more.

Use this work-ing book in whatever format you desire. Activities and questions can be completed daily, every few days, or weekly. However, the commitment to doing something for yourself is to be consistent to create the habit of taking care of you. Prioritize *you* every single day, whether it's for five minutes, an hour, or a full day. Commit to doing something that feels good and brings you joy. It is, without a doubt, the quickest way to reconnect with yourself and feel whole.

You can do this by yourself or invite a partner to join you in this process. A small or large group of friends could greatly benefit from committing to this experience together. While the focus is to support yourself, sharing with others is motivating and enriching, and helps with accountability. It also reiterates the simple truth that we are all in this together. No matter what is going on, we could all use some extra support and love.

However, you choose to engage with this book will be perfect for you. It's time to connect with you—on your terms and in your way. And here's the hidden bonus: the more you practice taking care of yourself and doing what you enjoy, the more you will feel better about your life and who you are. When you experience joy, it increases not only your mood but also your realization of the good around you. It allows you to see with more clarity the positive parts of living, even in the middle of what does not feel good.

Living serendipitously is allowing your life to be what it is while noticing and embracing the unexpected joy that shows up. Live in the flow of what your life is reflecting to you. As you open your eyes to what is in front of you, you can begin to appreciate just how beautifully orchestrated life is to give you what you say you want. When you recognize that your part is simply to create opportunities for you to feel good, the easier it will become to let the unexpected ones stream into your awareness. This recognition is what gives you the proof that the more you support yourself, the more life supports you right back.

Sometimes living in the flow serendipitously means letting the discomfort and pain rise up and out. While our desire may be to avoid these feelings, they need to be felt and expressed. The relief after a hard cry or a loud screaming fit (ideally to yourself) is a huge release that cannot be compared. After you've freed yourself of emotions such as these, a space is created for you to receive the surge of clarity and peace you've been craving! The longer you push them down, the longer they linger. Living is allowing life and your feelings to be what they are and supporting yourself in the process of experiencing them.

Start noticing the good that exists effortlessly. It could be as simple as getting to work on time with no traffic or setbacks, or enjoying a few moments to yourself in solitude in a day you thought would be too busy to sit down. It could be positive interactions with your family or friends, or receiving help from somewhere you wouldn't have guessed. Anything that brought you even momentary satisfaction or joy. Commit to creating more opportunities for joy as well being open to receive them.

In addition to doing something for yourself each day for the next thirty days, commit to writing down what brought you joy, whether unexpected or intentional. What good things happened? What was meaningful and special about your day? Did you live in the flow or resist? Live serendipitously. Live your life as it's meant to be—filled with unexpected joy and experiences designed in your favor.

You can write down these reflections at the end of the day or the following day if that's how you choose to use this book. Write as little or as much as you want to hold on to. Do whatever works for you to stay consistent. The proof you will create for yourself that life is amazing and miraculous is too good to pass up.

Everyone wants life to "taste" good, and we often look for recipes to spice things up. At the end of this book, you will have created a unique and personalized selection of "spices" that you can go back to time and time again if you begin to feel the symptoms of disconnection and depletion creep back in. The spices don't go bad or expire. They are your reconnections to your joy, readily available to be added when life tastes bland and unsavory. You will have created your own internal support with a how-to guide. Self-awareness and an action plan simplified. And fun! Connecting with yourself is as amazing as you allow it to be. Get excited! Your life is about to change for the best.

Day 1

*Most of the shadows of this life are caused by
standing in one's own sunshine.*

—Ralph Waldo Emerson

One of the biggest setbacks you may be currently facing is feeling lack of joy in your life. You may easily know how to take care of others, but when it comes to you, you feel stuck on even where to begin. That changes starting today!

We need to add more joy into your life and have you rediscover all your awesomeness waiting to be expressed and experienced. We will do that by starting with a list of what you like to do or think you may like to do. And you, in turn, will commit to doing something on this list, every single day. In addition, I want you to begin noticing what good things happen to you each day as well without you even trying. This will give you the proof that your efforts will continually pay off the more you focus on your joy—whatever it looks like.

Think of this process as dating yourself, getting to know and support yourself as you are. When you start dating someone, you spend time listening to them and understanding them. You try new activities and adventures together to see what they enjoy. You want to see them smile and like to see what makes them happy. You also notice the things they do for you or the way they make you feel without expecting it. Sometimes that keeps you even more interested in getting to know them and what's going to happen next.

This is what you will start doing for yourself. Let's discover even more about you and what it is that lights you up and makes you feel alive. Let's add more fun and lightness into your days and remember how good it feels to smile and laugh regularly. This is your opportunity to do more of what you love and less of what you don't!

I want you remembering what it's like to have fun! And I also want you being open to the awesomeness that's already around you.

When I created my list, it was all over the map. It ranged from trying new foods, connecting with friends, taking long walks in the woods, practicing meditation, and doing a puzzle with my kids.

When I had more time, I would drive to the ocean or sit by a river or stream nearby. I planned dates with friends and dates with myself, and I spent time with family.

On busier days, I made sure I did something simpler to bring joy to myself like treat myself to fresh flowers in my living space or look up inspirational phrases that shifted my thoughts. My funds were limited, and if yours are too, focus on adventures and opportunities that are more about experiences and opening your mind than on buying things or activities that are costly.

I did, however, choose to spend money on myself, because it was part of me supporting and loving myself the way I would for someone else. I bought an empowerment outfit, went on an empowerment mini vacation, and had several empowerment dates with myself. All my activities focused on doing what I wanted to do and what felt good for me. It elevated my appreciation of the importance of doing little things, and how each of those small gifts added up in my bank of self-worth, value, and feeling connected to myself.

As my resources have grown, I have expanded what it means to do for myself. When I feel doubt and wonder if I should put an idea on the back burner because it is too costly or time-consuming, I practice pushing through those old beliefs and doing it anyway. I have yet to experience an ounce of regret when I support myself and enjoy the process.

Now it's your turn.

What are the types of activities you enjoy? Or once enjoyed and put aside? When life felt more carefree, what were you doing with the time you had to yourself? If you are struggling to remember or feel like you don't know what you enjoy any longer, survey people you know. Ask them what they enjoy doing or passions they have discovered. You may get some ideas you hadn't thought of or inspiration to try something new.

Create Your Joy List

This is your time to explore you and learn or relearn who you are and what you like. Enjoy your own company and that which ignites the joy and passion in your life. You can keep adding to the list as ideas come to you.

Make a list of at least thirty things you can do that bring you joy or feel supported. Once you start, it will get easier.

They can be as simple as

- going for a walk;
- sitting quietly with your coffee or tea for five minutes and breathe;
- reaching out to a friend and talking about what's on your mind;
- watching a movie you really enjoy;
- dancing as if you were born to;
- learning something new that interests you;
- writing your thoughts in a journal;
- signing up for a class to learn something new;
- singing in your car or anywhere in your home as loud as you can;
- taking a nap in the middle of the day;

- planning a vacation you've been thinking about;
- painting with all the colors of the rainbow;
- taking a relaxing bath;
- listening to your favorite music;
- starting a creative project;
- rearranging a room in your home; or
- reading an inspiring book or quote.

Add in extra external support of your choice as well, such as taking a yoga class, getting a massage, inquiring about receiving an energy healing, and so on.

It may feel like a lot to get started, but it will get easier, and it will also be enjoyable. Trust me on this one. Now let's get started and create some joy together!

1. _____

2. _____

3. _____

4. _____

5. _____

6. _____

7. _____

8. _____

9. _____

10. _____

11. _____

12. _____

13. _____

14. _____

15. _____

16. _____

17. _____

18. _____

19. _____

20. _____

21. _____

22. _____

23. _____

24. _____

25. _____

26. _____

27. _____

28. _____

29. _____

30. _____

Today's Reflection:

What brought you joy, whether intentional or unexpected? What was meaningful or special about today? Did you live in the flow or resist? How did you live serendipitously? _____

_____

_____

_____

_____

_____

_____

Day 2

Faith is not belief. Belief is passive. Faith is active.

—Edith Hamilton

When life becomes challenging, one of the quickest ways to manage stress and worry is to look at your core beliefs about life and living. Do you believe that there is a power greater than you? What do you call it? Why do feel the way you do? What do you believe and trust?

If you believe that you are protected in life, then you can let go of the fears of being harmed. If you believe that you are given what you need, then you can release the fear of lack. Identifying your core beliefs reminds you of the foundation you've grown from and the roots to return to when you are in need of grounding and support.

I believe in a power greater than myself and that I am supported by this power throughout my life. I believe that everything happens for a reason, and each of my experiences are designed to benefit me in some way. I believe I can learn and grow from my choices and their outcomes, and I believe I have the power to change my thoughts, beliefs, and behaviors whenever I choose.

I also believe that essentially everything works out in my best interest. I am safe even when my mind and the illusions of my fears attempt to rattle me.

I believe I am unconditionally loved and cared for, and my job is to relearn and remember this and share that same love wherever I go. And I also firmly believe and trust that the more I live by my core beliefs, the more enjoyable and serendipitous my life is.

I did not always believe this. I grew up attending Christian churches and questioned just about everything at different points in my life. I questioned why "bad" things happened to "good" people and why it was hard to trust something I couldn't see. I questioned the meaning of life and the purpose for our existence. I questioned the occult, the presence of God and the devil, the definition of "good," and where on earth I fit in to any of it.

Over time, and with lots of prayer to whoever I thought was listening to me, I was led to books and teachers who echoed what, underneath my fear, felt true. I believed in something bigger and bolder governing life; I just wanted proof that it was real. One experience after another presented itself in my life that solidified my views and beliefs. Even though I could never see what I felt, it appeared in a way that was meaningful and valid. I received the proof I asked for.

Most things I feared did not come to be, yet if they did, I learned something important by living through that fear. People showed up in my life when I needed them most. Answers to my questions found their way to my consciousness. If I lost something valuable, it was replaced with something even more meaningful. This is how my core beliefs became my foundation. And the more that I have faith, the more I am given opportunities to both challenge them, practice them and accept them as truth for me.

Now it's your turn.

You may have been taught what you believe or you may have developed your beliefs on your own through experience. This is a great time to get clear about what they are. Let them not just be your guide moving forward, but the place to fall back to when you are in need of support. The positive vibe of Faith and Trust will soothe your soul whenever you tap into it.

Core Beliefs Question

What are your core beliefs? What do you believe is the purpose of life? When you think of faith, where does yours lie? How does this belief dictate your decision making? How does it support you when you are under duress? Define not just what your core beliefs are, but why they are yours.

_____

_____

_____

_____

_____

_____

_____

_____

_____

_____

_____

_____

_____

_____

_____

_____

_____

_____

_____

_____

_____

_____

_____

_____

_____

_____

Today's Reflection:

What brought you joy, whether intentional or unexpected? What was meaningful and special about today? Did you live in the flow or resist? How did you live serendipitously? _____

_____

_____

_____

_____

_____

Day 3

Expose yourself to your deepest fear; after that,
fear has no power, and the fear of freedom shrinks
and vanishes. You are free.

—Jim Morrison

D o you find yourself worrying often about the future or getting stuck in a thought train of guilt, wishing you could change the past? Do you daydream about what it would be like to be free of the feeling of being stuck?

You are not alone.

If you look at the phrases people are drawn to—"be free, live free, roam free, talk freely, free to be"—the sense of freedom plays a strong role in our ability to feel balanced and content.

When we don't feel free, symptoms of anxiety creep in when we feel trapped in our minds and in our circumstances. We recycle the same thoughts and feelings that become familiar in their repetitiveness and find it difficult to let them go. Yet freedom from the internal oppressiveness is exactly what we are craving, wherever that oppression is derived from.

Identifying what you view as freedom allows you to see where you feel restricted, as well as where you can break free and feel the freedom you desire.

For me, freedom means no constraints, not being tied down and restrained. Most of where my freedoms have been lacking have been in my mind. I desire to be less bogged down by needless worry. The evolved part of me understands how there is nothing to worry about, how my needs are consistently taken care of, but my long-standing habit of angst-filled thinking is stubborn and crafty. When one thought is reasoned with, another one pops up to question why it's not being heard.

When I first answered these questions, I felt I needed more freedom in the ability to choose how I live my life. In order to have those freedoms, I had to make different choices in where I put my time and attention on a daily basis. I altered the way I saw myself living, and my reality changed with it. I wanted more time to spend on myself, so I made it a priority.

I wanted to create a work schedule that met the needs of my family, so I made decisions and boundaries that adhered to them. It was uncomfortable to make some of the adjustments when I first began. I feared I might not make enough money to pay my bills, or I'd put so much focus on myself that other people in my life might feel neglected. Neither of those fears came to be. In fact, the more time and attention I gave myself, the more elevated my mood rose and the more energy I had to put into my family and my responsibilities—guilt-free.

Since I now comfortably live in that lifestyle, my sense of freedom has expanded. The deeper I go, the more I see that freedom is a practice of letting life flow in the direction it's designed to, without me attempting to stop it. When I breathe through the changes in my thoughts, emotions, and experiences, I feel unrestrained, which releases my anxiety and worry, and lets my sense of balance be restored at a quicker pace.

Freedom for me also means to speak my truth. When I censor my thoughts to protect myself from the judgment of others, I am, in turn, judging myself. By holding back, it's as if I believe what I think and feel is wrong. Yet if my intentions are not to harm, why am I so afraid to share how I really feel? I had to look at this too. Whose judgment am I trying to free myself from, and what is really my ultimate fear?

It turns out it was, and still can be, rejection. At times I feared if I allowed myself to be vulnerable and exposed, I would be rejected and alone, reminding myself that I am not, in fact, good enough. Those self-doubts are agitating!

The paradox? What I have found is the more I give myself the freedom to express my truth, the less weighed down I feel, and the more comfortable I am with myself. The more I expose my heart and my beliefs and take ownership for them, the more I love myself. Quite the opposite of negative self-judgment. Life is funny like that, isn't it? What we think is scary is actually what gives us the most peace when we look at it for what it really is.

Now it's your turn.

Looking at where you desire more freedom in your life will give you a sense of where your current constraints are. What do you feel is blocking you from your joy? Where do you feel stuck?

Freedom Question

What does freedom mean to you? What does it feel like? Where would you like more freedom in your life, and how can you create it?

_____

_____

_____

_____

_____

_____

_____

_____

_____

Today's Reflection:

What brought you joy, whether intentional or unexpected? What was meaningful and special about today? Did you live in the flow or resist? How did you live serendipitously? _____

_____

_____

_____

_____

_____

_____

_____

Day 4

Those who think they have no time for bodily exercise
will sooner or later have to find time for illness.

—Edward Stanley

How good are you about moving your body? How do you view exercise? Is it on your list of "I used to" or "I should, but I don't" or "Ugh, no thanks"? Or do you feel the noticeable benefits of regular movement? I'm going to push you on this one because it is just that important.

Exercise in any form is the best anti-anxiety and anti-depressant around. Moving your body and getting the blood, thought, and energy flow going is incredibly healing.

You know how you feel when you've been stagnant for a while, and you know how you feel when you get your body moving. Everything changes. And then you say, "That felt good."

Movement creates an important shift in our energy, and it also helps us be more present in the moment. One of the first homework assignments I give to my clients is the practice of forward movement and no longer standing still. Our bodies want to support us in that movement, and it is our responsibility to support it back.

It is exceptionally therapeutic as it balances our brain chemistry feeding us "feel good" chemicals and derailing the stress-inducing ones. If you want scientific proof, it's one internet search away. If you want your own proof, get yourself moving and note how differently you feel. I simply can't recommend it enough.

I have always been a physically active person. I have a lot of energy, and I experienced a great deal of anxiety as a child and felt the need to move to burn off the excess energy and stimulation. As I grew older, I noticed a huge difference between when I was active and when I wasn't. I learned early on that it was a necessary part of maintaining my emotional well-being by supporting my body, which also supported my brain and emotional functioning.

I used to be drawn to high-intensity movement through running, heavy weight training, and high-impact sports, but as my life has changed, my preferences and needs have changed with it. I still enjoy high-intensity activities at times, but I no longer need them. My regular routines include walking and yoga and outside sports and activities with my kids.

When I have a lot on my mind and feel myself spinning, I make the space to go for a long walk. By the end I feel calmer and more centered, and many times, I find a resolution to my issue, which often includes letting it go. Physically, it feels good, but mentally, it's a remedy I can't personally live without.

And movement is just that—moving. It doesn't have to be painful and sweaty to be beneficial. Yoga and stretching are amazing activities that the body and mind devours in appreciation. Sports of any kind are fun and uplifting, and there are more videos on the internet and through apps that can keep you company and help you stay motivated to keep going.

Now it's your turn.

How can you incorporate more movement into your life? If you're not doing anything regularly, what is getting in your way? If you find yourself making excuses, write them down and then follow up with solutions to make it work.

Physical Movement Practice

Today is the day to commit to moving your body and, in turn, enhancing your overall wellness.

Start with fifteen minutes a day of anything. Whatever you can commit to and enjoy, just do it. Create realistic goals of what you want to achieve and get started.

If you already incorporate exercise into your day, look at where you can add or balance the process, including some days to just stretch.

Our bodies crave movement, so why not nourish them and give them exactly what they're asking for?

What exercise will you commit to?

_____

_____

_____

_____

_____

_____

_____

_____

_____

_____

_____

_____

_____

_____

_____

_____

_____

_____

_____

_____

_____

_____

Today's Reflection:

What brought you joy, whether intentional or unexpected? What was meaningful and special about today? Did you live in the flow or resist? How did you live serendipitously? _____

_____

_____

_____

_____

_____

_____

_____

_____

Day 5

*When everything is moving and shifting, the only
way to counteract chaos is stillness. When things feel
extraordinary, strive for ordinary. When the surface
is wavy, dive deeper for quieter waters.*

—Kristin Armstrong

How often do you feel the need to clear your head and slow down for a bit? Have you heard yourself say, "I can't even hear myself think"? When life gets busy and overwhelming, you may feel the need to pause and regroup, but you may not give yourself the time to do so. You may feel so wound up that slowing down feels like a waste of valuable time, and you program yourself on autopilot—which is exactly when giving yourself the space to be still becomes important, if not imperative.

You've heard meditation is good for you. You may think it sounds intriguing, but you don't feel equipped to stick with it. The benefits of meditation are well documented, as are the struggles most people feel when they attempt to start. The problem is not the idea of meditation but the expectation we create around what we think meditation "should" be.

I had been an avid wannabe meditator for years before I truly began my practice. Initially I tried guided meditations, lots of them. I listened intently and found it very relaxing. But eventually, my mind wandered all over, and I felt like I was doing it wrong when I couldn't get myself to focus.

I moved onto mantras, silently chanting powerful words and sounds to ward off those pesky villains of thought I referred to as my jabber-jaw mind. But, man, they were loud. Not only would they not stop chattering, but they were also speaking just as loudly as the mantras in my mind, competing for attention. They were really no different than my children trying to outperform each other. They expected me to give them equal amounts of focus, while I knew they secretly wanted to dominate the other, and I was forced to choose. Because of this, I found it difficult to hold onto the mantras when my needy thoughts didn't want to be silenced. It wasn't my meditation regimen of choice.

Unwilling to give up, I decided to try something new for myself; I practiced sitting still for five minutes. I gave my thoughts permission to come and go and rant if they chose to. I decided to stop judging them and let them be.

At first, I squirmed and peeked at the clock every minute, maybe even thirty seconds. I wondered how long I could last. As time went on, the experience became easier and more enjoyable.

What this did was allow me to get more comfortable sitting, and for longer periods of time. Telling myself I didn't have to focus actually helped me to focus more—on being still. Without judgment, my thoughts naturally began to slow down with less need for attention. Eventually, they even generated some really fabulous ideas, seemingly out of nowhere!

I asked questions and let the answers come to me on their own. Giving myself the time and space to be still allowed me the openness to hear what I was saying, or what was being conveyed to me, and ingest it. The practice of slowing down became essential in my healing process and in meeting my need to be heard and understood, judgment free.

If you are anything like me when you feel inspired, you try the techniques you think you are supposed to be using, and then you feel discouraged when your busy thoughts won't shut off. You wonder why you can't get it "right." This often goes one of two ways. You either judge the process, deem yourself a failure, and abort the practice in order to not feel worse about yourself. Or you accept that like with any skill-building process, you can decrease the harsh judgment and praise the ever-so-little successes of even trying.

Now it's your turn.

I feel passionate about the benefits of this practice and strongly urge that it be part of your daily routine. You may find yourself forgetting or making excuses as to why you can't. This is also part of the process of change. It is very easy to get in your own way and create resistance. Writing down the reasons you can't and then following up with why you can may be helpful.

This is a practice you can't get wrong as long as you give yourself permission to start and keep going. I assure you that with commitment, meditation and stillness is an incredible practice that can insert instant peace into your life when you are ready to receive it.

Create a Stillness Practice

Starting today, set aside five minutes each day to close your eyes and sit quietly. Set a timer if you need to. During these five minutes, your thoughts will flow in and out. Give them permission to flow and give yourself permission to be still. At the end of the five minutes, feel free to list three things you are grateful for. This will end the practice on a positive note, encouraging you to commit to it.

_____

_____

_____

_____

_____

_____

_____

Today's Reflection:

What brought you joy, whether intentional or unexpected? What was meaningful and special about today? Did you live in the flow or resist? How did you live serendipitously? _____

_____

_____

_____

_____

_____

_____

Day 6

*Miracles are a retelling in small letters of the very
same story which is written across the whole world
in letters too large for some of us to see.*

—CS Lewis

Have you ever experienced a miracle? I am certain you have.

Miracles are not just major events with flashing lights, so we notice them as the whole world changes in front of our eyes. They are the gentle whispers of love, the aha moments, the feelings of peace, the reminders that we are never alone and that we are always cared for.

Some people call them messages from the universe, coincidences, uncanny events, and serendipitous moments. Often they are referred to as answered prayers and timely good fortune.

How do you define a miracle?

I see them as the welcomed gifts we receive that are signs and reminders of just how supported we are. They occur daily, yet we are often so wrapped up in our thoughts, concerns, and plans that we miss what is right in front of us.

I'm not even sure I believed in miracles when I was a child, but I am now convinced they were all around me. It wasn't until I began to practice increasing my awareness that they seemed to multiply.

I have experienced many miracles in my life, and they have all been special. Beyond seeming to have exactly what I need show up in my life precisely when I need it, it's the symbolism in nature around me, hearing someone say the words that answered the question I had been thinking about all day, the feeling of peace washing over me after I pray, and sometimes beg, for reprieve. It's the ability to feel people's thoughts and emotions and the insight to look underneath the layers of fear.

It was the day my stocks rose two weeks before I was scheduled to buy my house, which I previously couldn't afford, giving me more funds than I thought I needed. It was the time I dragged myself to an energy-therapy class, feeling completely devastated with sadness after my first night alone and how I left with more energy, optimism, and excitement for life after learning how to channel the healing energy all around me.

It was the time I was thinking about someone I loved saving me as I drove down the highway, and two trucks drove by with the person's name on one and Knight (as in knight in shining armor) on the other. It was when a wrapped gift showed up at my office from an anonymous source, revealing a carved angel that looked just like my friend who had died, who I had felt with me the entire week before.

Miracles are simply everywhere. Whether we notice them or not, they exist.

Now it's your turn.

One of the homework assignments I give those who are ready for change is to notice miracles that happen to them and for them. I wish I could share with you the numerous stories I hear that highlight the amazing events and experiences when people become aware—from "chance" meetings to songs on the radio that match their thoughts and opportunities that seem to come from nowhere. It's a fun game to live in the flow of miracles!

Start opening up your eyes and your mind. Start to ask for miracles or signs or reminders to show up in your life and make themselves noticeable. Enjoy it!

The magic of life is unlimited. You get just as many chances and miracles as the next person. The more you open yourself up to their reality, the more supported and acknowledged you will feel.

Miracle Question

How do you define a miracle? Do you believe they happen easily or do you feel you have to earn them? What miracles do you want to occur? How often do you ask for them? What would it feel like to ask for more? How can you open yourself up to expecting more miracles in your life?

Ask for miracles to show up and begin to notice the magic that's around you.

_____

_____

_____

_____

_____

_____

_____

_____

_____

_____

_____

_____

_____

_____

_____

_____

_____

_____

_____

_____

_____

_____

Today's Reflection:

What brought you joy, whether intentional or unexpected? What was meaningful and special about today? Did you live in the flow or resist? How did you live serendipitously? _____

_____

_____

_____

_____

_____

_____

_____

Day 7

That was the thing about the world: it wasn't that things were harder than you thought they were going to be, it was that they were hard in ways you didn't expect.

—Lev Grossman

I know you are "should-ing" on yourself. I can feel it. I do it too.

"I should do this. I should do that. This should be happening, not that!"

They come from our expectations, and they are big. Our expectations can weigh us down and create obstacles everywhere we go. When not met, they can deplete the enjoyment of our experiences if we are unable to go with the flow.

Expectations are the pressure we put on ourselves to think, act, and be a certain way. The higher our expectations are for ourselves, the higher they are for the other people in our lives. It becomes a reflection of what or how we think things should be.

The weight of my expectations is an area I am continually adjusting. I was raised to be independent and responsible, and I am comfortable following through on that. However, sometimes I'm looking to do more and give more than is healthy for me.

After my divorce, I asked my ex-husband what was one of the biggest challenges he found being married to me. He answered immediately, "Your expectations." While he was referring to how I was tough on myself and how hard it was to get me to see my way out of it, I also knew I put a lot of pressure on him to be what I wanted him to be, as opposed to accepting him unconditionally as himself.

I didn't meet my own expectations. Therefore, I was going to find it nearly impossible for him to meet my expectations of him. And I blamed him for it. I didn't see my role at the time. His answer gave me the perspective I was looking for to understand what it is like to be close to me from the outside.

As a parent, I also find I have to keep my expectations in check when it comes to my kids. I think it's common to view our children as an extension of ourselves, and parenting is essentially teaching them our view of the world. I have to remind myself that they have various teachers in life, and they are not meant to be mini versions of me. And while my kids are strongly influenced by me, they have their own ideas and visions that don't look like mine. Accepting them for who they are, fostering their senses of unique awesomeness, and accepting it's not about me are critical to letting go of the responsibility I feel for meeting all of their needs. It's an ongoing check, for sure.

Now it's your turn.

When you have expectations of how you think other people "should" behave, it often sets you up for some big disappointments, especially when those people have no idea what your expectations of them are. When people meet your expectations more, you tend to like them. However, when they don't, they start to get on your nerves. Don't be surprised if what you don't seem to like about them is also something that you do yourself. It's an unpleasant little trick our minds play to remind us of our perceived shortcomings.

Many of your expectations were taught to you by your caregivers. If your parents or the people who raised you or who you admired were hard on themselves, they likely taught you to be the same. They may have put pressure on you, and you learned how to put pressure on yourself. These pressures become habitual and part of the way you think, and sometimes you don't even notice how much you are allowing them to weigh you down.

Sometimes your expectations come from being disappointed by your caregivers or people who influenced you, and wanting to be better than them at just about everything. You may put pressure on yourself to be stronger, more responsible, calmer, more loving, more open, more accepting—whatever you felt they were deficient in—to prove it's possible to be better and to make up for what you believe they lacked.

Recognizing your expectations and where they come from is the first step in awareness. Listening to the way you talk to yourself and the way you talk to others can be very eye opening. You can see how many heavy, expectation-driven words you use (*should, need to, have to*). Sometimes they feel so ingrained in your vocabulary that it seems impossible to adjust, but just like everything else, a little practice goes a long way.

Expectations Question

Where do your expectations come from? Whose voice are they? What expectations are blocking your joy? How are your expectations hurting you? How are they enhancing your life? Where can you gain more balance by altering your expectations? How will you be able to stick to this change?

_____

_____

_____

_____

_____

_____

_____

_____

Today's Reflection:

What brought you joy, whether intentional or unexpected? What was meaningful and special about today? Did you live in the flow or resist? How did you live serendipitously? _____

_____

_____

_____

_____

_____

_____

Day 8

Abundance is not something we acquire.
It is something we tune in to.

—Wayne Dyer

When we think of abundance, we tend to get very excited. Why? Because the opposite of abundance is lack or not enough—and the feelings of lack and not enough scare us.

If we focus on what we want, it's usually more of something. When we think about what we don't want, it's typically less of something.

What do you want more of?

I've noticed that the word *abundance* feels more meaningful when I feel depleted in some area of my life. When I step back and look at what I want more of, it's typically time, focus, and joy-filled experiences. Occasionally I also feel like I would like more resources in money and help. Since I sometimes feel lack in those areas, I look at what it is that I am doing or not doing to create the feeling of not enough. In short, the answer is my perception.

When I tell myself I don't have enough, I begin to feel discontent and unappreciative. I expect that I should have more or be doing more to attain this distant vision of happiness. I almost always lose sight of what I already have in front of me that is filled with abundant bliss.

I look at what I have control of and what I don't have control of. Do I have a way to create more time? No, but I can decide how I want to use the time I have to meet my needs and desires.

Do I have the ability to create more focus? Yes, if I prioritize where I put my attention and reduce some of the distractions I put in my way.

Do I have control over how many joy-filled experiences I have? Absolutely. I can make decisions to add more people, activities and adventure into my life and let go of some the obligations that aren't a priority.

Can I create more money in my life? Yes. I can work more or find new ways to bring in income that I enjoy in other areas I am drawn to. Can I receive more help? If I ask for more help, I can certainly receive it. It's the asking part that I usually hold back on, and that is something I surely have control over.

Being open to abundance is not just recognizing what I can do, it's also being open to receiving and feeling grateful for all I've already been given. I know the more I feel gratitude, the more open I am to receiving more to be grateful for.

Now it's your turn.

When you examine the word *abundance*, what is it you want more of? This puts you in the mind-set of looking at and structuring your life and decisions around what you want versus what you don't want.

When looking at what you want, it's helpful to ask what you are in control of to obtain it. Is it a matter of restructuring your priorities and where you put your energy? Or does it require more faith that your efforts are and will continue to pay off?

Before answering the abundance question, take a few minutes to recognize what you do have in your life and currently feel grateful for. Then look at the areas where you find yourself wanting more.

Abundance Question

What does abundance mean to you? What does it feel like? Where would you like more abundance in your life? What areas do you feel lack? What steps can you take to change this? Abundance, of course, is not just material, but so much more. It can be abundance of time, of freedom, of being oneself, of positive energy, of contentment. Abundance is a feeling that brings great joy.

_____

_____

_____

_____

_____

_____

_____

_____

_____

_____

_____

_____

_____

_____

_____

_____

_____

_____

_____

_____

_____

_____

_____

_____

_____

Today's Reflection:

What brought you joy, whether intentional or unexpected? What was meaningful and special about today? Did you live in the flow or resist? How did you live serendipitously? _____

_____

_____

_____

_____

_____

_____

_____

_____

Day 9

Embrace your differences and the qualities about you that you think are weird. Eventually, they're going to be the only things separating you from everyone else.

—Sebastian Stan

If you had to save the world and it was all up to you, how would you do it? What is your superpower?

We all have one. To be fair, we all have numerous skills, but there are at least one or two that we excel at. Is it your ability to feed a room full of people with few resources or your creative flair that makes any space look amazing? Do you sing like an angel, make music that could serenade an angry bear, or entertain people with your quick wit? Are you an artist who can bring emotions to life through your creations? Maybe you can negotiate any deal or have a heart that glows with innate kindness and people melt in your presence. What is it you do best?

It has been a long-running joke with my friends that I will talk to just about anyone. Sometimes I swear I can't help it. I cannot count how many times I go into a store or an event, sure that I just want to avoid people, and yet find myself talking to the next person I see. It seems nearly impossible for me to keep to myself. It's like a social reflex or something.

However, engaging with others is how I learn best about people. The more time I spend listening to others, the more my understanding of thought and behavior patterns is prevalent and clear. Which is exactly why this superpower will be the one I use to save the world from itself.

My superpower is the ability to make friends. I am certain that if I had to save the world, my tactic would be to befriend world leaders, help them see their innate insecurities, and how their fear-based decisions could be enhanced with a little perspective shift. I would instantly learn their likes and dislikes, and speak their language in a way I knew they understood. This is my gift. I have a deep compassion and understanding of people. Making friends and connecting with people is what I know how to do best.

It's also possible that my direct overanalysis of those world leaders would send them into quandaries of deep introspection. This would either have them resign from office once they see that their behavior is a danger to humankind, or empower them to see just how much positive change they can bring to the world. Regardless, it's my best tactic.

Now it's your turn.

You've got skills. What are they? If you were to ask your friends and family members what you do best, what would they say? What do people rely on you for?

Superpower Question

Identify your superpower and what it is you do to enhance the world and make it a better place. Be clear about why this is your superpower and how it benefits you, but also others. How do you use this superpower, and do you feel like you could use it more? If so, how? If not, why? Have fun with your superpower and the way you make the world awesome just by being yourself.

_____

_____

_____

Today's Reflection:

What brought you joy, whether intentional or unexpected? What was meaningful and special about today? Did you live in the flow or resist? How did you live serendipitously? _____

_____

_____

_____

_____

_____

_____

Day 10

Men are not afraid of things, but of how they view them.

—*Epictetus*

Fear. Friend or foe?

Right away most of us would likely say foe because we don't like the discomfort that fear brings us. But if we are learning to accept all of ourselves (psst, we are), fear is an excellent communicator to teach us something valuable.

If you are feeling fear, your body and mind are telling you something, and your job is to listen, not to respond right away, but to listen. Fear has a strong voice, a voice that sometimes protects and a voice that also blocks our potential joy. It's our job to practice listening and determine what is being conveyed.

Fear has been a consistent companion to me for most of my life. Fear talks to me a lot. I continue to practice listening to what it wants me to know and how it influences the course of my life.

While I was contemplating some big decisions I had to make, I reached out to a friend, telling them I was scared. I knew I had to make some adjustments, but the fear was fierce. I couldn't decide. Both options had a ton of obstacles, some internal (emotional and mental), some external (physical and financial logistics), and they felt about equal in weight.

My friend replied, "Take the fear out and then decide."

This has turned out to be one of the best pieces of advice I've ever received, and has become the base question of all my major decisions, as well as many minor ones! If fear didn't impact me, what would I do?

By taking out the fear, by eliminating concern and perceived obstacles (most of which will never come to be), I am able to look at my choices through my heart and intuition, and let them guide the way.

When my friend suggested this, I immediately asked myself which decision I would make if nothing could go wrong. The answer came quickly. And boldly. They always feel bold.

Most of the time, my answers feel empowering, because I know they are the direction I want to go in. But then my old pal fear creeps in and says, "Are you sure about that?"

So I continue to practice taking the fear out.

I take the fear out by listing my what-ifs and then replace them with the opposite what-ifs. For example, start with "What if I fail and can't follow through?" and turn it into "What if I succeed and am more proud than I've ever been?" Or "What if I go broke and have to sell all my belongings?" to "What if I make more money than I thought possible?" Or "What if I feel alone and unsupported?" to "What if my people rally behind me and I feel even stronger?" And my favorite: "What if 'they' judge me negatively?" to "What if 'they' are inspired by me to do the same for themselves?"

Now it's your turn.

Taking the fear out allows you to see your visions and hopes for what they truly are. It removes the angst-driven voices of the ego long enough to let the inner voice of knowing step up and dominate. The voice of courage speaks the truth, and you know the truth because you can feel it. The truth feels freeing, not scary; loving, not demeaning.

This is a great way to determine where your heart wants to go, but it's important to remember it's a practice. You can ask once and get your answer, but fear is persistent. It will return and ask to be heard again. This is okay. It is expected. The conversations will be continuous and lengthy at times. This is how you get to know your fear best and how to work with it and through it.

Eliminating the Fear Question

This activity is a focus on facing fears and taking risks. If you look back on your life and think about the risks that you've taken and the fears you've faced, the hardest part was not actually taking the risk, but the anticipation of taking the risk.

The fear comes from the perceived potential setbacks. It's just the idea of them that scares us, not the reality.

If you take the fear out, if you live in a magical world where nothing can hurt you, what would you do? Who would you be?

The greatest fears do not come from taking the risk to move forward, but from standing still.

What does your life look like when you take out the fear of moving forward and live the life you truly desire? What risk can you start taking today to get there? Do one thing that scares you and write about how you worked through it. Let this be a guide of how to keep going and engage your strength and courage.

_____

_____

_____

_____

_____

_____

_____

Today's Reflection:

What brought you joy, whether intentional or unexpected? What was meaningful and special about today? Did you live in the flow or resist? How did you live serendipitously? _____

_____

_____

_____

_____

_____

_____

_____

Day 11

Some people grumble that roses have thorns;
I am grateful that thorns have roses.

—Alphonse Karr

Be grateful. Give thanks. Think positively. Fill your life with gratitude for everything in front of you, and life will be wonderful. We hear this promise all the time.

Yet what if you struggle to feel grateful and joy-filled for what you have? How can you feel grateful in a moment when all you really want to do is whine because you just don't feel content? Sometimes the fact that you don't feel grateful makes you feel guilty that you're not as happy as you "should" be and then you really think something is wrong with you.

Do you ever feel bad because you don't feel as thankful for your life and your opportunities as you think you should? And then beat yourself up because you can't even get gratitude down right?

Ah, the human experience. I get it.

I have been called an eternal optimist many, many times. And it's true. I think I really am. I can reframe just about any situation to find the positive spin and meaning from it. I don't know if it's a gift or a survival tactic, but I have been working on it for some time now. One of my most deeply treasured confidantes, someone who knows me best, once said, "No one works at being happy more than you." I wasn't sure how to take it at the time, but I now recognize the truth in that statement. I absolutely work at it. My default mode is not to be perpetually happy, nor could I be if I tried. But I do put a lot of effort in making my life as enjoyable as I can. I cannot imagine doing anything less than that.

When my mother took her life, I had a lot of fear around how people would judge me based on her actions. I knew they would think I would be a mess and blame her for it. And because I felt very protective of her and myself, I made a conscious decision at age fifteen that I would do something positive with my experience. I knew I had a choice, and I refused to go down without a fight. I fought not to let myself fall into a depression, and I pushed through years of anxiety, always trying to find a way to manage it.

So when it comes to feeling gratitude, it has not come naturally to me. I work for it. That may sound odd, but it's my truth. I can list off a thousand reasons I have to be grateful, but that does not mean I feel the gratitude for them by just knowing what they are. I have to sit with it and let myself feel it, and it takes focused effort.

If I write or say the words, I let myself feel what they mean. If I'm thankful for the sunshine, I let myself feel warmth of it in me and the cold when it's not. If I'm thankful for my health, I let myself remember what it feels like when I'm sick to know the difference. If I'm thankful for being able to pay my bills, I let myself recall what it was like when I felt like I couldn't. I feel the dark and the light, and I am grateful for both to give me the full experience to know what joy and true gratitude feel like.

When I stick with it and ingest the feeling of gratitude, it's a high like no other. It feels much better to put in the time to feel the good than to automatically think of the reasons why I could be angry, sad, or upset. The simple switch in brain chemistry alone is worth the effort.

This is why I know identifying and feeling the reasons you have to be grateful is particularly important. I strive to do this every day to give myself a boost and remember why I do what I do. It's a practice that consistently rewards me with a feeling of contentment and appreciation and switches off the autopilot thoughts of seeing the void and questioning how I will fill it. And it is, truly, a practice.

Now it's your turn.

You know the difference when you feel grateful and when you are just saying the words. Recognition and listing them out may seem easy, but feeling it may require more effort. The good news is, you know how it feels, so it's just a matter of accessing that feeling and letting it linger. You know what discomfort and unease feels like, and you know what relief feels like. Bring up the feeling of gratitude you've experienced and notice how it escalates and grows the longer you sit with it.

Gratitude Question

Nothing can change us like the power of a thought. No matter what's going on around us, our thoughts control our moods and our perceptions of our experiences. Every thought creates a chemical reaction in our brain, which creates a physiological response in our bodies. No person, event, or drug can impact us the way our thoughts do.

Gratitude is a thought at its highest vibration. Gratitude exudes love, honor, and respect, sensations we strive to maintain.

Today, make a list of thirty things you are grateful for and why. Anything! List out what feels good about what you are grateful for. Notice how it feels when you focus on the positive and notice how long it lasts—or doesn't. This will give you an awareness if you are countering your experience of feeling grateful.

Life is amazing and filled with gifts if we allow ourselves to accept them. Practice noticing them today and have fun with it!

1. _____

2. _____

3. _____

4. _____

5. _____

6. _____

7. _____

8. _____

9. _____

10. _____

11. _____

12. _____

13. _____

14. _____

15. _____

16. _____

17. _____

18. _____

19. _____

20. _____

21. _____

22. _____

23. _____

24. _____

25. _____

26. _____

27. _____

28. _____

29. _____

30. _____

Today's Reflection:

What brought you joy, whether intentional or unexpected? What was meaningful and special about today? Did you live in the flow or resist? How did you live serendipitously? _____

_____

_____

_____

_____

_____

_____

_____

_____

_____

_____

_____

_____

_____

Day 12

Worry never robs tomorrow of its sorrow,
it only saps today of its joy.

—Leo Buscaglia

Worry is generated from a fear of the unknown. When we don't feel in control and we want to do more to influence a situation, we often employ worry as a means of mentally directing how something is going to go. We question what-if in every angle to feel as though we will be prepared. We are looking for proof that things are going to work out, and we try to safeguard ourselves when we fear they won't.

What is fascinating is that we spend an incredible amount of time filling our heads with anticipatory anxiety, and then we are pleasantly surprised or completely relieved that our fears did not come to fruition.

Worry is a habit of thinking. That's it. Most of us have been trained to worry by our parents and caregivers from an early age, or we've somehow developed a belief that life can't be trusted and, even worse, that our senses and feelings can't be trusted, because what if we are wrong?

This is why turning around and looking for proof can be helpful in curbing current and future worry. Writing a letter to your younger self to give yourself advice, encouragement, and understanding allows you to see not only how far you've come, but also how important all those lessons were, the ones you deemed positive as well as the ones you felt have challenged you.

When I wrote this letter, it was eye-opening to see just how much I've changed. Taking risks, being uncomfortable, and shaking up my old patterns have been some of the best things I've ever done for myself. Writing to my younger self, who worked diligently to balance her old worry habits along with engaging with her new pal, Faith, deserved to know that her tears and frustration would lead her to new heights she had yet to see.

I wanted her to know that the dedication she felt in her bones was important and she would reap the benefits even though the darkness looked awfully daunting for a while. I wanted her to know she was supported and not alone. It felt great to write and even better to confirm one of my core beliefs: everything always works out.

Now it's your turn.

Isn't it great to know that most of what you obsess and worry over rarely comes to fruition? And like most people, you are looking for proof of this fact. Luckily, that proof is available. When you turn around and look back at the times you worried and questioned the future, where you made all your predictions of what could go wrong, how often did those fears comes to be? I know. Barely ever.

And even the ones that did, what gain came from them? What positive outcome came from what you believed was going to be life-shatteringly negative? And how much time and sleep did you lose swimming in the fear of what would never come to be rather than appreciating what is real and valid now in the present moment?

When you look back again at those challenging times in your life that were heart wrenching and painful, would you have chosen them if you knew they were going to happen? Maybe or maybe not.

If you knew the painful parts and outcomes of all of the decisions and events in your life that were meant to help you grow, you could easily choose to avoid all the discomfort that leads you to even more sustainable joy and happiness. However, you would lose the opportunities that taught you your greatest strengths and allowed you to face even more fears to become the most courageous version of yourself.

This is a great opportunity to look at your past and remind yourself how your experiences have molded you into the amazing person you are now. Not only is it a great practice to remind you now, but also it's a great reminder for the future you. No matter what happens next, you've got this.

Letter to Younger Self

Think of all the time you've spent worrying about things that never came to fruition, while holding your breath hoping life would get easier. In truth, no matter how much time you spend worrying, generally everything works out.

Write your younger self (five years younger or even six months) a letter. Give yourself all the advice you wish you knew and share the wonderful things you've learned.

_____

_____

_____

_____

_____

_____

_____

_____

_____

_____

_____

Today's Reflection:

What brought you joy, whether intentional or unexpected? What was meaningful and special about today? Did you live in the flow or resist? How did you live serendipitously? _____

_____

_____

_____

_____

_____

_____

Day 13

*There is no passion to be found playing small -
in settling for a life that is less than the one you are
capable of living.*

—Nelson Mandela

I AM.

These are powerful words. Whichever words we add after them will be how we define ourselves. Whether in the moment or overall, I AM is the prefix to the version of ourselves that we perceive.

It's so important to give ourselves the space to look at ourselves and define what we see. We often say, "They don't know me," in our heads, so this is your opportunity to say who you are, where you've been, what you like, and what you don't like. They all make up the very beautiful being that is all encompassing you.

As for me,

I AM a mother first. I AM loyally invested in my family. They are the staples and strength of my life.

I AM a friend and confidante to all who invite me in.

I AM a counselor of life, a writer, and a storyteller.

I AM the kind of person you want to be friends with, because I will make you laugh and support you, but I AM also the person who will annoy you when I call you out or when you find my perspectives too deep for your liking.

I AM a truth seeker, an empath, and a goddess in my own right. I AM an optimist 85 percent of the time, but a pessimist when I'm cranky and I can't seem to find my way.

I AM passionately in love with words, emotions, and all the complexities that come with them.

I AM brave, but I live with more fear than I ever disclose. I AM an overthinker who has to push myself through every ounce of self-doubt that has followed me around since early childhood.

I AM extremely sentimental, and I cry at all of my kids' events, whether a band concert, open house, or blowing out candles on a birthday cake; they all do me in.

I AM a lover of beer, good food, traditions, sunrises, and every ocean I've ever stood next to. I AM a stargazer, and the one who will never pass up a good campfire as the headlining event.

I AM deeply compassionate, as I feel all the discomforts and patterning of our insecurities. I AM one who easily forgives, because anger is my least favorite emotion.

I AM someone who loves and who wants to be loved. I AM just like you.

Now it's your turn.

Who are you? What are the qualities you like most about yourself? What are your strengths? What are the parts of yourself you would like to feel more compassion toward and need more love?

This is your opportunity to summarize who you are. You can do this with I AM statements like I did or write a few paragraphs to describe who you are. You can also do this with pictures or art or phrases or quotes or anything that feels like it depicts who you are. Have fun with it!

Biography Question

This activity is a focus on how we see ourselves and how we want others to see us. If you had to give a three-minute summary of what you are all about, what would you say?

Write a brief biography of the you that you could share, no more than two to three paragraphs, or write a list of who you are. Or if you'd prefer, create your biography in any creative way your heart chooses. What makes you unique? What do you bring to the table? Who are you in this world of ours? So much.

_____

_____

_____

_____

_____

_____

_____

_____

_____

_____

_____

_____

_____

_____

_____

_____

_____

_____

_____

_____

_____

_____

Today's Reflection:

What brought you joy, whether intentional or unexpected? What was meaningful and special about today? Did you live in the flow or resist? How did you live serendipitously? _____

_____

_____

_____

_____

_____

_____

Day 14

The beginning of love is to let those we love be perfectly themselves, and not to twist them to fit our own image. Otherwise, we love only the reflection of ourselves we find in them.

—Thomas Merton

One of your struggles may be your interactions with other people. The way you find yourself treated by others or your discomfort with the way you treat others. You may find some of your stress coming from friendships or family dynamics or your romantic relationships. It's quite common.

Relationships with others, all relationships, are our greatest lessons in self-love and acceptance. How we view ourselves is often directly associated with how we are treated and what we believe about ourselves.

Even though we are told that it is not important what others think of us (and that really is true), it's fair and honest to acknowledge that we struggle to accept this fact, and most of us still crave the outside validation of our worth. It's as if we are human or something.

How we view ourselves has a profound impact on our relationships with others. Like still attracts like, and our reflection is a fabulous teacher.

In a relationship, I had always been a giver. I gave all of myself. If my loved one had a problem, it then became my goal to solve it. I would think of nothing else until I knew the person I cared about was okay. It was consuming.

And I absolutely thought it was my responsibility. I would tell you it wasn't, but my actions and focus proved otherwise.

I was the epitome of a people-pleaser. I would put everyone else's needs over mine, and I would be exhausted at the end of each day doing my best to make sure everyone around me was "happy." And if I got one small inkling that perhaps someone didn't like me or was going to reject me, I would reject them first to protect myself.

Turns out, that long-standing pattern does not work well in building and maintaining strong relationships of any kind. It also didn't work out well for me where it started: with my own mother, whose mental illness threatened her presence in my life, and began my pattern of fear and withdrawal.

After my divorce, when I made the effort to figure out what it meant to love myself, I also had to learn who I really was and why I was repeating the same patterns. Learning these aspects of myself has become the main ingredient for self-acceptance and compassion—for both others and myself.

I learned that giving all of myself is exactly what depleted me to the point of not even being sure of who I was. My internal journey and identification of my patterns taught me what I wanted to tweak and where I, in fact, was a master. I backtracked to see exactly where my patterns began, as well as my insecurities and my sense of self-worth. I gotta say: it was absolutely fascinating.

So now, in a relationship, I have a great sense of who I am, what I want to give, and what I want to receive. This allows me to be the most authentic version of myself and not compromise my own value and worth.

Now it's your turn.

Looking at how you interact with others and how you feel about the interactions will give you an idea of how you see yourself. How you allow others to treat you and the way you respond are great indicators of any type of imbalance in your sense of self-worth.

Relationship Question

Who am I in a relationship? What do I give? How do I give? What is it I want in return? How do I express love? In what ways can I express love more to others? In what ways can I receive more love?

How can I give more love to myself and enhance my relationship with me? What are action steps I can take to make this happen?

How will you honor yourself and, in turn, your relationships today?

_____

_____

_____

_____

_____

_____

_____

_____

_____

_____

_____

_____

_____

_____

_____

_____

_____

_____

_____

_____

_____

_____

_____

_____

_____

_____

Today's Reflection:

What brought you joy, whether intentional or unexpected? What was meaningful and special about today? Did you live in the flow or resist? How did you live serendipitously? _____

_____

_____

_____

_____

_____

_____

Day 15

Tradition is not the worship of ashes, but the preservation of fire.

—Gustav Mahler

You know that feeling where it seems like everything is changing and yet nothing has changed at all? It's a safe and comforting feeling, when you celebrate a favorite holiday or birthday or a traditional event that you look forward to, the feeling of nostalgia and warm memories, but also rooted in the present moment when life feels good right now. I love that feeling.

Holidays, traditional or self-created, and the traditions that accompany them are wonderful. Traditions become a memory scrapbook of how much we change and yet stay the same, no matter what is going on around us. They represent the constants in our ever-changing worlds. We use them to feel connected to the past and to celebrate the present.

I have always been a huge fan of traditions. Being raised by someone with mental illness did not support a stable environment for me. Because my mother was emotionally impaired and my father worked a lot, I clung to anything that felt like it would stay the same in my life, since I rarely knew what to expect next most days.

This is where our traditions fit in. During my childhood, we hosted Christmas Eve dinner at our house, no matter who was able to join us. I always had electric candles lit in my windows, which for the month of December soothed my fear of the dark.

For our birthdays, we always went out to dinner, and we got to choose where we wanted to go. During the summers, my brother and I stayed with our grandparents in Maine for two weeks. We swam, fished, hiked, played board games, and had lobster parties on picnic benches with instructional how-to-eat-a-lobster plates and nut crackers that were generations old. They were our traditions, and they always stayed the same no matter what was going on in the rest of our lives. Those traditions made me feel secure in my not-always-secure little world.

Establishing traditions for my own children has been of the utmost importance to me. We have never missed Christmas Eve dinner at my father and stepmother's house, and we always have electric candles lit in the windows of our home for all of December and January. My kids' birthday celebrations include their taking the day off from school and me from work to celebrate however they choose.

We still go to Maine for vacations with our family, and we still have lobster parties on picnic benches with instructional how-to-eat-a-lobster plates and nut crackers generations old.

In addition, we are often creating new traditions for ourselves, for the simple reason that they are fun. And we have a thirst for more fun.

During my *30 Days to Me*, I created Family Bacon Day on the last day of June. I do not eat red meat or pork (due to a thirteen-year-old obsession with actor River Phoenix, a vegetarian) and, therefore, do not eat bacon. But my kids do, and they love it. In an effort to create an outside-the-box tradition, we eat bacon on the last day of June, and I must say, it is delicious! In fact, I ate so much bacon that first year I questioned why I ever gave it up (RIP, River Phoenix)—until the next few days when that same bacon sat in my stomach to remind me. Note to self: less is more.

Now it's your turn.

What do you like about traditions? What could you use more of? If you're looking for a way to add some spice to your life, create a tradition that feels exciting and one you'll look forward to. Traditions can be anything! Let yourself be as creative and fun as you want. Enjoy the break from the everyday, and do something special you'll want to build off for years to come.

Create a Tradition

This activity is a focus on traditions and making life fun. Finding a reason to reform the mundane into something magnificent is one of the joys of living.

What are your favorite traditions and why? Create new traditions just for fun. Shake things up, make today special just because you can.

What new tradition will you create?

_____

_____

_____

_____

_____

_____

_____

_____

_____

_____

_____

Today's Reflection:

What brought you joy, whether intentional or unexpected? What was meaningful and special about today? Did you live in the flow or resist? How did you live serendipitously? _____

_____

_____

_____

_____

_____

_____

Day 16

The beginning of wisdom is the definition of terms.

—Socrates

Do you have any catchphrases you are drawn to? A favorite quote you like or motto you live by? What is it about the words that keep you coming back to it? Words are powerful—the ones we read, speak, and feel. They are also something we have complete control over in how they are used by us.

We have the opportunity to choose our words every moment of the day and the way we deliver them. Because there are so many options, we don't have to limit ourselves to the same old patterns and choices. We can reshape ourselves and the way we communicate with one simple decision: choose the words that feel good. Taste them before you serve them. So simple and so effective.

They feed our psyche, and depending on how we digest them, they create our present realities, our futures, as well as our abilities to heal our pasts.

I am completely in love with words. They each have a powerful vibration and weight, both audibly and in our minds and bodies, creating waves of sensations that structure the flow of our emotions and, in turn, our moods.

In my old life as a school counselor, I co-created and facilitated an antibullying program for adolescents. The name of the program was the Power of Words. Teenagers shared their stories of pain to younger schoolmates, exposing the dangers of causing harm to others with words.

I sat with them through their tears of recalling the torment of being pummeled by harsh words. Those who bullied with words felt just as much sadness and angst as those who were on the receiving end. The awareness of the words they used and the intentions behind them was transformative. They learned together that words are equally powerful, whether they are used as weapons or as instruments of love.

I am acutely aware of the words I use and how I use them. I feel them as they come out, and because of this, I pause before the hard hitters make it to my tongue or are written out. I know how strong they are.

I also know just how heavy my expectations and self-judgements are by the words I use to describe my needs. I feel the pressure I put on myself with the amount of "shoulds" I use each day. I also recall the names I've called myself and put-downs I've owned. I know what it's like to be your own worst enemy. Yet I also know how amazing it feels when I pick myself back up and cheerlead myself through challenges using uplifting and positive words to boost my mood and drive.

Now it's your turn.

Do you feel the weight of your words?

Words like *hope, love,* and *faith* raise you up and allow you to breathe with ease. Whereas *should, hate,* and *need to* bring a heaviness and lower your energy and flow.

Want some proof?

Close your eyes and say the word *hope*. How does it feel? Now try the word *love*. What do you notice in your body? Say the word *trust*. This could have an interesting reaction.

Say the word *should*. Where do you feel it in your body? Next, say the word *hate*. What does that feel like? Try the word *no* and see what changes you encounter.

Pretty cool, isn't it?

Since words are a tool you use to communicate to yourself and others, it's helpful to see how you are using these tools. Recognizing which words you use on a regular basis can tell you a great deal about why you react and respond the way you do.

For example, replacing *hate* with *makes me uncomfortable*. Or *I can't* to *I feel challenged by* or *I don't want to*. A big one is *I need to*. Replace this with, *I'd like to*, or *it would benefit me to*.

I absolutely feel the difference when I say *I should* versus *I'd like to*. Do you? Pressure words are my go-to defaults. I put a lot on myself. Yet when I notice what I'm doing, I can also stop, reevaluate, and revamp my expectations.

It becomes easier with practice, but the result in feeling is immediate. The weight of words is significant, and a few adjustments can absolutely go a long, long way.

Word Usage Recognition

Notice which words you frequently use today and the impact they have on your body and mood. You have the ability to change them whenever you choose.

Write down the words you find yourself thinking and saying the most, along with the feelings associated with them. Which words would you like to use more? Which words would you like to replace or alter? What do you notice about the frequency of the words you use?

_____

_____

_____

_____

Today's Reflection:

What brought you joy, whether intentional or unexpected? What was meaningful and special about today? Did you live in the flow or resist? How did you live serendipitously? _____

_____

_____

_____

_____

_____

_____

Day 17

The ache for home lives in all of us, the safe place
where we can go as we are and not be questioned.

—Maya Angelou

Dorothy said it best in *The Wizard of Oz* when she reminded us, "There's no place like home." If you could click your heels together and be anywhere, where would you be? Who would you be with?

When you've heard yourself say, "I feel at home here," ask yourself why. What is it that feels good to you? Why is it comforting?

Home to me is where I feel comfortable in my own skin. It's where I don't censor my words or my feelings. It's when my voice sounds more passionate, open, and loving, and when I am at ease exactly where I am at the moment. I breathe with more fluidity.

It's when and where I trust myself the most. And when I fully trust myself, I trust the environment around me. I trust the people I'm with, the place where I let my feet feel settled, even if only for a short time. It's where I want time to slow down so I can savor where I am. When I feel connected to who I am and feel my inner light glow, I know I am home.

There are certain people I feel at home with and specific places I return to that feel safe and familiar. But I've also noticed that it starts with me and how connected I'm feeling to myself at the time. If I go away on vacation for a week, I can make myself comfortable in my surroundings and get cozy, but I also look forward to going back to the life I've created that I feel good in. When I return to my house, I notice that I almost have to rediscover myself there to get comfortable again. This is how we adjust ourselves to our surroundings and how we nestle into our comfort zones. I love my space and my things, but I also like to explore myself in other places and find myself there as well. I like to find my home within me so I can bring it anywhere.

Now it's your turn.

If home is a sense of comfort, safety and familiarity, where do you feel yours? Looking at what home is to you can give you deeper insight into your comfort zones, where they are and why. This also allows you to identify when you're not comfortable and steps you can take to feel more at ease.

Home Question

What does home mean to you? Where is your home? Is it a place, is it a feeling? What does it look like? What are you doing when you feel at home? What is surrounding you? Who are you with? How do you know when you are home?

_____

_____

_____

_____

_____

_____

_____

_____

Today's Reflection:

What brought you joy, whether intentional or unexpected? What was meaningful and special about today? Did you live in the flow or resist? How did you live serendipitously? _____

_____

_____

_____

_____

_____

_____

Day 18

*Today's accomplishments were yesterday's
impossibilities.*

—Robert H. Schuller

In this busy life where we sometimes forget the purpose of everyday living, it can be easy to lose sight or forget what we've done and where we've come from. We focus on our to-do lists rather than our done lists, and we put our energy into filling the gaps instead of recognizing our completeness.

Taking time to turn around and see what you've accomplished, what you feel good about, and where you've met your own expectations is extremely valuable in identifying your strength and endurance, as well as seeing that life supports you when you support yourself.

Personally, I am gifted at placing high demands and pressure on myself toward what's next instead of recognizing the present moment or the wake of awesomeness I've left behind. It's a practice I've been working to alter for several years.

During a time that I was feeling particularly down and struggling to find gratitude in the everydayness of my life, I began a new practice of noticing the daily events and interesting occurrences. I started to keep track of what gifts I experienced each day by writing them down the next day after reviewing it.

This practice helped me realize what great things happened each day of my life, as well as showed me how what I thought was challenging often led to something wonderful.

I began to see the positives of my life more readily as they were happening. But more importantly, identifying my accomplishments proved the value of my efforts and experiences. They ignited my belief that everything had a purpose and power to it, whether I saw it in the moment or not. It increased my confidence that the work I had been doing on myself was paying off and my progress was continuous.

Recording the daily occurrences proved there truly is an accomplishment in each day and each moment when we let ourselves see it. It showed me that life is serendipitous in our everyday living, and the more we take note, the more we can trust this truth. This is also why this practice is included in this book.

Now it's your turn.

How often do you turn around and see what you've accomplished? Do you focus on the gap of where you are now and where you want to be instead of how much you've already done?

When you give yourself the credit you've earned for making the tough decisions, for reaching the goals you once established, for maintaining balance in chaotic situations, and sometimes just enduring the painful moments of life, you create an opportunity to see just how valuable you are. And powerful. And strong. And accomplished.

It's important to note your successes not just over time, but in everyday living. Reminders are often the ideal boost to keep the momentum flowing.

Accomplishment Question

Focus on your accomplishments. Where have you been and how far have you come?

Make a list of your accomplishments in the past year as a reminder of how your visions become your reality when you choose to make them so.

What have you accomplished that you set out to do? What have you accomplished that you didn't set out to do? What are the gifts that have come from these accomplishments along the way?

Today, feel the pride of knowing what you bring to the table and congratulate yourself for embracing your awesomeness.

_____

_____

_____

_____

_____

_____

_____

_____

_____

_____

_____

_____

_____

_____

_____

_____

_____

_____

_____

_____

_____

_____

_____

_____

Today's Reflection:

What brought you joy, whether intentional or unexpected? What was
meaningful and special about today? Did you live in the flow or resist? How
did you live serendipitously? _____

_____

_____

_____

_____

_____

_____

Day 19

You always have two choices:
your commitment versus your fear.

—Sammy Davis Jr.

When you are asked to make a commitment, how does it feel? Do you find it easy to say yes and guarantee your presence and your energy? Or do you hesitate?

Maybe you find it easy to make promises because upholding them is important to you. Or maybe you like to get more information before you put yourself in a position to potentially disappoint. How are you at making decisions? Do you trust that any perceived mistakes you may make will teach you something, or are you fearful of being of wrong?

True confession: I had a major fear of commitment when I first did this. Major.

Commitment felt like containment to me, and I did not want to be contained. It wasn't until I deciphered the difference between the two that I realized I actually commit to living most days of my life.

Prior to my divorce and leaving my secure job, I had every weekend and holiday planned for a year in advance. I mapped out where I would be and what I would be doing. My mood or circumstance rarely had a role in my planning. I just made plans and stuck to them.

After my divorce, I was hesitant to commit to much of anything. And after I left my job to start my business, I didn't know what my future would hold. My commitment fears were overblown. I kept hearing myself say, "I don't know what my life is going to look like in one month, let alone one week. I can't commit."

In reality, I was struggling to trust myself and make promises since the previous commitments I once made did not end up the way I expected or hoped. I gave up trying to predict what was going to happen next. However, I knew I didn't want to disappoint anyone in my path. I went from a "yes girl" to a "maybe girl." And those "maybe girls" used to drive me nuts.

At some point I realized my moodiness and indecision were becoming a bit overbearing and preventing me from living my life the way I wanted to—with conviction, determination, and commitment to whatever I put my energy into.

It was then I knew I needed to start with the most important commitment: to myself.

Therefore, I made a list, a list I have hanging in my home and in my office so I see it daily, a list of commitments I don't want to lose sight of.

- ~ Commit to Something You Love
- ~ Commit to What Makes Your Heart Sing
- ~ Commit to What You Know You Want and Deserve
- ~ Commit to Speaking Your Truth
- ~ Commit to Faith
- ~ Commit to Love
- ~ Commit to Living
- ~ Commit to Feeling Whole
- ~ Commit to Supporting Yourself
- ~ Commit to an Idea

- Commit to a Feeling
- Commit to Letting Go of the Past
- Commit to Not Giving Up
- Commit to Not Walking Away
- Commit to Sitting with the Discomfort
- Commit to Knowing the Uncomfortable Feelings Are Temporary
- Commit to Forgiveness
- Commit to One Step, Every Single Day
- Commit to the Vision
- Commit to the Breakthrough
- Commit to the Joy
- Commit to Knowing It's Happening

Now it's your turn.

When you commit to what you believe in, what you feel in your heart, you are committing to you. Dedicating your energy and focus to yourself doesn't just enhance your life—it shows others how important it is to take care of themselves.

When you commit to feeling good, the people in your life will benefit, the planet will benefit. We want you to feel good so we can feel good as well.

When you commit to yourself, know you help all of us.

Commitment Vows

Commitment: a promise to do something, to be there, to follow through, to stay; regardless of how you might feel. In so many ways, we commit easily, and in many ways not so much.

Today, write vows to yourself, a renewed commitment to honor, respect, support, trust, and love yourself unconditionally, a promise that you can rely on yourself and your beliefs no matter what.

_____

_____

_____

_____

_____

_____

_____

Today's Reflection:

What brought you joy, whether intentional or unexpected? What was meaningful and special about today? Did you live in the flow or resist? How did you live serendipitously? _____

_____

_____

_____

_____

_____

_____

_____

_____

_____

_____

Day 20

Darkness cannot drive out darkness; only light can do that. Hate cannot drive out hate; only love can do that.

—Martin Luther King, Jr.

When someone says to you, "You just need to forgive," what's your immediate reaction? Does your wall of defenses go up? Do you feel annoyed and resistant? Or do you recognize the power forgiveness gives you?

You may feel that if you forgive, you are no longer protecting yourself and you're setting yourself up for another round of grief. The anger you've built up and held on to may feel safe and strong. And while in the moment it may seem that you are mightier with your reinforced defenses, there are no lasting benefits to staying angry and resentful.

Forgiveness is one of the most empowering feelings we can experience. When we feel ongoing anger and resentment, it gives our power away to its target. When we feel forgiveness, we take our power back and feel more balanced.

Remember: we are not our thoughts and behavior. If we were, we each would have lost a lot of friends and loved ones along the way with mistakes we've made. We are the beautiful souls underneath the behavior. All of us.

I've always told my kids there is no such thing as a bad boy or a bad girl; there is only bad behavior. Behavior is an action, and we can always choose to change our thoughts and our actions when they make us uncomfortable. We are constantly learning and growing into the life we say we want, and so is everyone around us.

I will not preach to you that practicing forgiveness is easy. But I will remind you that the benefits are for you and you alone. I have been attacked, betrayed, hurt, and emotionally assaulted by various people and experiences throughout my life. I have felt the rage that comes with being put down and insulted, and I've questioned why on earth anyone would try to hurt me in the ways that I have been. I have also been the person who has hurt others. I have made decisions that I knew were not in my best interest and could potentially cause great harm to another person, but I did them anyway. My intentions were never to hurt, but they were not always to protect either.

I have been self-absorbed and inconsiderate and careless. And I have also been treated with disrespect and dishonor that shook me to my core and made me question myself and the safety of life. All have been opportunities for me to look at myself and reevaluate my thoughts, beliefs, and actions—and choose my response accordingly.

My experiences taught me not only the devastation of other people's actions, but the pressing guilt of my own. Both were equally painful, as well as beneficial. The feeling of anger toward others is no less uncomfortable than the anger we have toward ourselves.

This is why forgiveness is so powerful. Literally, full of power. It allows us to stand in a place where the anger doesn't hurt us anymore. When we identify ourselves and others as having a human experience and doing the best we can with what we have or know at the moment, we can engage more compassion and understanding that everyone is just trying to figure it out. Because it's true.

Now it's your turn.

When thinking about a person or experience that still upsets you, ask yourself, when do you feel like you lost your power? Where did you feel like a victim? Identify who and what you felt anger toward and betrayed by.

Then step back and look at what your role was. How could you have responded differently? What did you do or not do that had an impact on the situation? What could you have changed?

Imagine the person who hurt you is a small child who is vulnerable and defenseless. Most likely their behavior is coming from that protective little kid in them who also doesn't want to be hurt. They use the tactics they think are intimidating, forceful, or manipulative to get their way. And they may even seem to feel good that their tactics are working, on the outside. On the inside, they are scared and afraid that someone is going show them up and expose them for who they believe they really are, and it ain't pretty.

When we treat someone poorly, we feel the pain of it, just as much as when someone else treats us poorly. The internal angst is the same. Most people who harm others beat themselves up way more than those they harm. It's just how we are designed. It may not always seem that way, but people who are the most insecure are the ones who attack to the highest degree. They, too, are attempting to find their power.

This is not to say that harmful behavior is acceptable—you don't have to forgive a behavior—but releasing the attachment is a valuable freedom that will give you the relief you deserve. By engaging compassion, you don't have to feel the toxicity of the anger. And that is meant to help and heal you, no one else.

Forgiveness Question

What does forgiveness mean to you? What does it feel like?

Who do you need to forgive most in your life? Who is the first person that comes to mind? What, if any, are the resistances you are feeling toward forgiving?

Once you've identified the resistance, ask yourself what it would be like to let it go and be free? What have you learned from the past that you can take with you?

What are the steps you can take to feel peace around forgiving? How can you hold onto it?

Who will you forgive today?

_____

_____

_____

_____

_____

_____

_____

_____

_____

_____

_____

_____

_____

_____

_____

_____

_____

_____

_____

_____

_____

_____

_____

_____

_____

_____

_____

Today's Reflection:

What brought you joy, whether intentional or unexpected? What was meaningful and special about today? Did you live in the flow or resist? How did you live serendipitously? _____

_____

_____

_____

_____

_____

_____

Day 21

Honesty is the first chapter in the book of wisdom.

—Thomas Jefferson

It seems fair to speculate that all of us have withheld expressing our true thoughts and feelings at some point. Withholding our truth is a natural defense mechanism, and defense mechanisms are important. They are an instinctive means of protecting us.

As children, we are taught to engage filters of expression as a defense. When we vocalized something outside the realm of cultural courtesy and social acceptance, our parents, teachers, and role models quickly corrected us to "not say those things in front of people," and they hurried us along out of earshot.

Of course, there's nothing wrong with protecting others from what might be offensive; it's our nature to be compassionate. Yet less often are we taught an alternative or socially acceptable way to speak our truth and how we really feel. Early on, we learn to shove our true feelings down, because we are concerned someone might get hurt, and it might end up being us if we are rejected for speaking our truth.

So when and how do we learn to express our truths, if we are concerned with controversy and rejection? For most of us, it's trial and error. One day we hit our limit and spew out every truth, no matter how unpleasant, we've ever had. And then we are stuck doing damage control. At some point, we learn through our own reactions and the reactions of others what works and what doesn't work. But there are clear signs to know when you are speaking your truth and if you are doing it effectively.

How do you know you are being forthcoming and honest? When the words roll off your tongue and taste good. You know how you feel when you say what you really think, and then people thank you for your honesty. People are also drawn to you for advice when they feel you are being authentic.

You also believe your own words when you hear yourself speak what is real and valid. You feel like a whole person and not giving yourself away to make someone else feel good. These are distinct feelings that let you know you are comfortably speaking your truth.

I find myself often giving people a heads-up before I am about to call them out. I literally say, "Here's where I'm going to call you out." I want them to know I am listening and that I see discrepancies in what they are saying. I want them to know my intention is to help them and not to make them feel bad, although I usually only do this if they are looking for supportive advice or if I see they need help regaining their power and not playing the victim.

What has been more challenging for me is speaking up for myself. When I have strong feelings about something that impacts me and I want to say how I feel, I have to push myself to do so. If I feel it puts me in a position where I could be rejected or attacked, I am much more hesitant, and I find myself resistant to speaking up.

However, the more I push through this discomfort, the more I gain confidence in letting my heart express what feels right to me. Additionally, the high I feel afterward from facing those fears has definitely been worth the shaky pushes I keep giving myself. Like everything else, practice makes this easier every time.

Now it's your turn.

What were you taught about speaking up for yourself and expressing how you feel? How did this impact the way you share what is on your mind? Do you find yourself holding back expressing what you really feel in an effort to protect yourself and others?

If you look at the ways listed above to know you are speaking your truth, you will see that the more you trust yourself and have acceptance for who you are, the easier it becomes to communicate your needs and feelings. Typically, the only thing holding you back is fear. Once you identify the fear of saying what you mean and meaning what you say, you can work with it to move through it using the tools you have been learning in this book.

There is something extremely freeing about being able to share your authentic self to the world and the people you love. And oftentimes, it begins by expressing who you are and what you think. Today is the perfect day to get started!

Expressing Your Truth

This activity is a focus on honoring your truth and expressing it completely wherever you go and whoever you are with.

Practice speaking your truth. Whatever you are feeling and thinking, be honest. When you speak your truth gracefully and directly, you are treating yourself and those around you with the utmost respect and consideration. Even if it makes you uncomfortable, being honest is being authentic, and being authentic to yourself is the greatest expression of love.

When you are being true to yourself, you can never go wrong. You have the freedom to speak from your heart—let's get you using it!

What areas of yourself do you want to express with more honesty in your life? What's holding you back?

_____

_____

_____

_____

_____

_____

_____

Today's Reflection:

What brought you joy, whether intentional or unexpected? What was meaningful and special about today? Did you live in the flow or resist? How did you live serendipitously? _____

_____

_____

_____

_____

_____

_____

_____

_____

_____

_____

Day 22

*Patience is not simply the ability to wait - it's how
we behave while we're waiting.*

—Joyce Meyer

Waiting.

It feels difficult for so many, myself included.

The root discomfort of waiting comes from not feeling content in the present moment. What about the moment is uncomfortable? Why are you certain all the other future moments will be better if the one that is current, the only one that exists, is so uncomfortable?

When you are waiting for something you want, but you are enjoying where you are waiting, the wait feels bearable, easy, and even comfortable. We often want to be distracted by things when we are waiting to avoid the discomfort of being present. We have bars that offer us distraction while waiting for a table; toys and magazines available in the waiting room of professional offices; television and movies playing anywhere they can be streamlined in or downloaded to whatever device you own. We are not trained to sit still with our thoughts and our company.

We live in a culture that promotes immediate gratification. We want everything here and now, and when it's not, we get edgy and uncomfortable, wondering why it's taking so long.

But if we get comfortable and appreciate the space we are in, it doesn't make as much of a difference how long we wait.

Many people are not comfortable being alone. Therefore, they distract themselves with cell phones and tablets, keeping their minds preoccupied, filling the time making plans, filling the spaces, rarely sitting in quiet with just themselves. Yet when we are sitting with someone we enjoy, the time flies by and waiting seems like no big deal. We enjoy the company we are with. If you are uncomfortable being alone, you might ask what it is about your company that you are not enjoying?

I used to really dislike being alone. I felt as though I needed constant distractions. Fill the time, every moment, please. Sitting and waiting for just about anything felt like torture when I was by myself. My mind would race and obsess about wanting to be anywhere other than where I was.

When I got divorced and my kids spent time with their dad, it was my first real lesson in being alone. At first I was really scared that I would not handle it well. I didn't know what to do with myself, but I knew I wanted to get comfortable in this new space I was in.

I dedicated my time to discovering what it was I liked to do, and with that, I began to enjoy my own company more. I let myself move through the discomfort I felt by writing and reading, but just for me. I had more time to myself, yet I spent less time with friends. I also stopped writing the parenting blog for others that I had spent so much time thinking about as well. My focus was to be alone and get comfortable with myself.

The practice worked. I began to hear my own thoughts and enjoy my space. I filled my time with long walks, introspective thoughts, and sitting with my insights. I will not tell you it was easy. My edginess increased as I practiced being still. Because I like to feel productive, it was initially a tough sell to myself to do things I simply enjoyed for the sole purpose of appreciating my own company. However, once I found myself beginning to enjoy who I was, I realized just how important it had become for my overall well-being.

Now it's your turn.

When feeling impatient, it can be helpful to ask what it is about your current state, your present moment, that makes you feel uneasy? Where is the fear, sadness, edginess, coming from?

Practicing being present and taking in the moment can help release some of the discomfort.

Getting comfortable with being patient means finding ways to enjoy where you are, finding the purpose of the moments, and recognizing they are just as valuable as when you arrive at your intended destination. And if you have to look and scrape for reasons, do that. Thoughts of gratitude don't always naturally flood you when you ask for them. Sometimes you have to search and be open to let them in, and that's okay.

When you are enjoying what you are doing, time seems to fly by, and you don't want to stop. You may have these desires to bend time based on how you are feeling in the moment. The more you enjoy the moment, find the good in it, find the joy, find something to appreciate, the more you want to live in them: all of them.

Focus on Waiting

Waiting. What are the first words that come to mind when you think about having to wait for something? If there is discomfort, where does it come from?

Do you find it challenging to be patient? Why? Where do you feel your impatience comes from if you experience it? What are steps you can take to ease the discomfort when having to be patient and wait for something you want?

_____

_____

_____

Today's Reflection:

What brought you joy, whether intentional or unexpected? What was meaningful and special about today? Did you live in the flow or resist? How did you live serendipitously? _____

_____

_____

_____

_____

_____

_____

Day 23

What is joy without sorrow? What is success without failure? What is a win without a loss? What is health without illness? You have to experience each if you are to appreciate the other. There is always going to be suffering. It's how you look at your suffering, how you deal with it, that will define you.

—Mark Twain

You know that feeling you have when you are pulled in different directions and you're not sure which direction to turn? Your energy feels scattered and your ability to focus is diminished. Sometimes it's so overwhelming you want to boycott it all and do nothing. Yeah, that feeling. Imbalance.

Balance—the art of giving and receiving in equal parts. A marriage between work and play. We strive for balance in most areas of our lives, yet we often feel as if it's slightly out of reach, sometimes way more than slightly. It's helpful to note where you feel imbalanced, so you know where to put your attention. And be realistic about it. You cannot put your attention everywhere at one time. It doesn't work well.

I am constantly striving for balance as a single mom with a business and a house and a deep desire to help others, while having enough playtime to keep myself sane; it's a challenge.

What I've discovered is that when I am clear with my priorities and boundaries, it becomes easier to maintain balance. I take the power back in my life and own it.

One practice I began was to jot down what area of life I wanted to set as my focus for the day. It set the stage of where to direct my energy, as well as not put it on everything at once. This practice helps give me guidance, but also allows flexibility to shift if something comes up that requires my attention. I mean, this is life. It doesn't always go as planned.

I notice the more time I spend addressing my imbalances, the more productive I feel. This includes delegating responsibility as well as letting things go. I attempt to maintain balance in my daily habits by prioritizing my emotional and physical health first, then interpersonal connections, followed by what I would like to get accomplished in relation to my responsibilities and goals.

When I feel I have equal parts in motion, my energy flows, my ideas pour out, and inspiration seems to be part of the oxygen I'm breathing in. I see my life as running smoothly, and when bumps hit, and they always do, I am better equipped to navigate a rerouted course when I feel the overflow is balanced.

Now it's your turn.

A simple way to determine where you feel imbalanced is to ask where you are giving your energy versus where you are receiving? If you feel like your time is limited, look at where you are focusing your time and energy and where you would like it to be. Where you would like to put it is likely what gives you joy and remember, joy is the name of the game here!

The push to over-give often comes from a long-standing belief system that suggests it is better to give to others than to yourself. If you feel this way, ask yourself where this belief came from and if it is, in fact, true for you. If you feel you must always give to others first, ask yourself why and how that belief impacts you.

When you identify where your imbalances are, you can address them directly and either ask for more or give less to establish equilibrium.

Balance Question

Where are the current imbalances in your life? What do you have control over? What do you feel you don't have control over? How can you create more balance? And how can you sustain it?

_____

_____

_____

_____

_____

_____

_____

_____

_____

_____

_____

_____

_____

_____

_____

_____

_____

_____

_____

_____

_____

_____

_____

_____

_____

_____

Today's Reflection:

What brought you joy, whether intentional or unexpected? What was meaningful and special about today? Did you live in the flow or resist? How did you live serendipitously? _____

_____

_____

_____

_____

_____

_____

_____

_____

Day 24

For my part I know nothing with any certainty, but
the sight of the stars makes me dream.

—Vincent Van Gogh

There is something absolutely magical about nature, the self-sustaining properties of growth and regeneration, the way animals in the wild seem to effortlessly live and thrive, the smell of the sun warming the earth, or the crisp freshness of nighttime air. By the ocean, in the mountains, by a brook or lake, surrounded by trees, or in the vastness of open fields or desert, there is something stunningly beautiful about being enmeshed in nature.

I personally cannot explain its healing powers; I just know they exist. I know I feel very different being outside than inside, and when I can't be outside, to have windows or plants near me gives me the sense of life outside the walls around me.

Nature teaches us many lessons of how to live, by the look and feel of their gifts to us, by the messages the animals send us in their presence. Just by breathing oxygen that feels fresh and pure, there is beauty everywhere.

I walk outside as often as I can, and one day during a very trying time of my life, I decided to take a "gratitude walk." I focused on things I felt good about as opposed to all the misery I seemed to be putting all of my attention on. What was interesting was, as I looked around, I began to notice things I had not noticed before. Details that had likely been the same for the past two years I'd been on this walk, but hadn't seen.

I noticed how tall the trees were. They looked down on me lovingly with their wisdom and whispered their secrets of balancing the seasons of change. They had been rained on, snowed on, pushed constantly by wind, and lost their leaves every year, yet they continued to grow. They had withstood extreme cold and heat, been damaged by storms, suffered broken branches and lost limbs, while watching others be taken out to make room for new houses, yet they stood taller one year after the next.

They were strong and stable, and they made room for the new while the old fell away. Looking at them, you would not know how they sustained the cycles. They looked as radiant as ever. It reminded me of how strong we are as humans, but we don't give ourselves enough credit, often focusing on the weaknesses.

It helped me see how strong I was too when I recalled how much I had changed, by choice. The trees served as an incredible reminder of what I needed to know at that moment—that everything was going to be okay. I would withstand the intensity of the seasons. My strength wasn't going anywhere, and it served me well up until this point, just like the trees.

Animals in nature serve as amazing reminders as well. They often show up in our paths at exactly the time we need them. You'll be amazed if you do a quick internet search for the meaning of animals who show up in your life and what they want to tell you. They are fun little messengers of just how interesting our lives are!

Now it's your turn.

How do you feel while in nature? Do you notice a difference when you are inside versus outside?

What are some of your favorite places to be in nature, and how often do you go?

Think about the last few times you spent in nature or around it and the impact it had on you. Imagine the sights and sounds of the outdoors as you recollect your experience. Does it feel peaceful?

You could very well be in need of more nature in your life!

Appreciation of Nature

Nature has the most extraordinary healing elements, and they're free to you if you choose to accept them. Fresh air and fresh perspective go hand in hand. Being outside anywhere can be rejuvenating and shift your mood.

If you can't be outside due to extreme temperatures, allergies, or because you'll pass out if you see a bug, take the outside in. Bring flowers or plants into your space to feel nature's essence, or display artwork of nature that you are drawn to. Sit by a window and just take it in. Just feel it in whatever way works for you.

The activity of enjoying nature helps you to reconnect with yourself and to feel grounded. Make time today and every day to be in some element of nature or bring nature to you.

In what way can you incorporate more of the magic of nature into your life?

_____

_____

_____

_____

_____

_____

_____

_____

_____

Today's Reflection:

What brought you joy, whether intentional or unexpected? What was meaningful and special about today? Did you live in the flow or resist? How did you live serendipitously? _____

_____

_____

_____

_____

_____

_____

Day 25

Between stimulus and response there is a space.
In that space is our power to choose our response.
In our response lies our growth and our freedom.

—Viktor Frankl

We give our memories a lot of power despite the fact that they are just that—memories. They are stories of our past. Because they are stories, they no longer have form, yet we regularly give our focus and energy to them as though they are still happening. We relive the story over and over again.

We judge the memory as good or bad, and feel the emotions we once felt when they occurred. The power of our minds and what they can create is incredible.

Sometimes I think—okay, often I think—I came into this life to have specific experiences to understand them, and then help other people. And the reason I think this is because I often find myself in situations, listening to people talk about an experience I can relate to. My mind listens, my senses feel, I understand them, and then I think, "Aha! I get it. I know exactly how that feels"—through my filter of course. Those are the moments I feel gratitude for having had my own experience to understand, validate their feelings, see the road they're on, and shine some light on some of the darkness I know they're seeing. Not only does it feel good to have had a reason to experience my own discomfort, but I am also rewarded with the joy of being able to help someone else.

Now to be clear, I am rarely ever grateful in the moment when I am experiencing something painful. I do the "Why me?" "This again?" and "What did I do to deserve this?" trio. I squirm, I cry, and I look for all the ways out. I avoid, I run, and sometimes I even sprint, but in the end, I'm still stuck with the same agitating pains to be felt so they can move on.

At that beautiful point, when I've reached the end of the roller coaster I didn't realize I'd actually stood in line to wait for, I marvel at what an incredible ride it was—jolting, terrifying, not sure if it would ever end, but always with some sense of "I conquered that!" once I get off.

Now it's your turn.

Since you have the power to recreate these stories and give them weight and control over your current decisions, you also have the power to create new ones, brand-new stories, brand-new experiences, anytime you want.

You have a choice to sit in the gap of where you wish you could have changed the story, or you can change the story's meaning.

Giving yourself the opportunity to reflect on the gains of an experience you deemed "bad" is taking the power from it to impact you negatively. It allows you to see how your heartaches and devastations gave you something that you didn't even know you wanted or needed until you had it.

It may have been gratitude for what you have, or letting your heart feel deeply enough to see how much it mattered. It may be that you didn't know you had the inner strength to cope until you had to, and found resources within yourself to do so. It could be that your patterns were becoming so ingrained, that your routine had to be shaken up so you could change what you were doing. Sure, sometimes the gifts are challenging to receive, but that doesn't take away from the fact that they are gifts.

Painful Memory Question

Choose a painful memory—the first that comes to mind. How has this experience blocked you? How has it taken control of your life? How can you take your power back so it no longer hurts you? What would your life be like if you filled the experience with gratitude for what's been learned instead of fear? Who will you be when you let the negativity of it go?

Today, choose to let go and grow.

_____

_____

_____

_____

_____

_____

_____

_____

_____

_____

_____

_____

_____

_____

_____

_____

_____

_____

_____

_____

_____

_____

_____

Today's Reflection:

What brought you joy, whether intentional or unexpected? What was meaningful and special about today? Did you live in the flow or resist? How did you live serendipitously? _____

_____

_____

_____

_____

_____

Day 26

Setting goals is the first step in turning the invisible into the visible.

—Tony Robbins

Identifying where we see ourselves and where we want to see ourselves is one of the most important steps in change and progress. We are naturally good at determining where we don't want to be, but often forget to look at the value of the rest stops before we hit our destination.

Without those rest stops, we would be uncomfortable, tired, achy, and feel very little reprieve. They also give us a place to stop and reevaluate where we are headed, and determine if we are taking the best route.

Starting with an end goal and working backward to see our rest stops, planned and unplanned, can help us stay on track and keep our motivation up.

When looking at your goals, it's helpful to not just write them down, but to feel them. Think about and feel where you want to be and work with the feeling. What is the goal feeling behind your intended result?

How do you feel now and how do you want to feel? Identifying how you currently feel gives you a sense of where you are and where you want to head. It's helpful for you to know why you want to feel differently and how you will know if you have "arrived."

Feeling goals are fabulous markers for all goal setting, because most of the time what we are chasing is a sense of security, value, peace, balance, independence, acceptance, connectedness, or self-worth. The decisions we make and expectations we set revolve around how we want to feel when we get what we desire. Whether it's a new car, house, job, relationship, health improvement, habit change, skill-building, or enhanced communication, we are looking for the feelings that come with it.

When you identify the feelings you are striving to live in more consistently, you can work backward to determine what you believe is getting in the way of those feelings. It's important to recognize which feelings need to be addressed or managed in ways that better support you instead of holding you back.

As I was setting goals for myself, one that I struggled with was to be in a balanced, interdependent relationship. I kept finding myself wanting this in my life, yet something seemed to get in the way. I was making efforts to improve my relationships, but I kept finding myself in the same cycle of disappointment.

It wasn't until I sat in the feeling of being in a stable, balanced, and committed relationship and imagined what that would look like that I noticed I had a real fear attached to it. When I sat in the fear a little longer, I recognized the guilt that was under the fear, and the fact that I didn't actually feel like I deserved positive relationships and partnerships. It was my buried feeling of lack of self-worth that was actually holding me back, as well as a fear of attachment and abandonment.

My words were adamant that I wanted healthy relationships more than anything. I mean, I'm a mental health therapist for goodness sake! However, my actions quietly sabotaged this "truth." I made decisions that blocked me from what I said I wanted, and most of the time, I didn't even realize it. It wasn't until I kept ending up with the same feeling and worked backward, that I discovered it was me getting in my own way the whole time.

Now it's your turn.

When making goals of what you want, identify the feelings that come with it to determine what it is you'd like to achieve. Additionally, notice any other feelings that pop up, trying to argue against it and tell you why you can't or shouldn't have it. This can be helpful in understanding why you are getting more of what you want or more of what you don't want.

Where do you want to be and how will you know if you are heading there? How will you feel once you've arrived at your goal?

Spend some time looking at and feeling what you say you want and why.

Goal-Setting Question

Take time today to update the personal goals as well as professional goals you have been thinking about. This will help assess where you're at and what direction you want to head in. Include three to four subgoals for each goal that will show you are on the path you desire.

The most ambition we feel comes from the vision of living in our passion. Spend some time thinking and feeling where your passion lies, as well as what generally inspires you to feel good. Let this be your guide when generating your goals.

Note also how you will feel if you reach these goals, and any fears or apprehension that may come with it. Also identify where any excitement or relief comes from and why.

_____

_____

_____

_____

_____

_____

Today's Reflection:

What brought you joy, whether intentional or unexpected? What was meaningful and special about today? Did you live in the flow or resist? How did you live serendipitously? _____

_____

_____

_____

_____

_____

_____

Day 27

The best love is the one that makes you a better person,
without changing you into someone other than yourself.

—Unknown

If you are a natural overgiver, there's a great chance that spending time devoted to yourself is not a regular occurrence. In fact, the idea may sound dreamy, but when given the opportunity to do whatever you want, you're not even sure what that could be.

When was the last time you had a day to yourself doing exactly what you wanted to do and only what you wanted to do?

If you're anything like me, spending a day with myself was a foreign concept. I still remember when my kids went to their grandmother's house for a few hours each Mother's Day. It felt like the ultimate gift to just have some time alone with no responsibility. My long walks felt luxurious, and being in a quiet house alone was almost too good to be true.

When I realized I needed to get to know myself, really know myself to love myself completely, I decided to start dating myself to find out what I was all about. The concept alone felt like a wild discovery.

The first date day I ever had with myself, I called out sick from work and went for a drive. I headed toward a quaint little town I'd discovered on my way to one of my daughter's soccer games. I had so much on my mind. I was in the middle of a divorce, trying to understand what I was doing and where I was going, and I felt totally overwhelmed. The drive alone felt freeing.

The town had several restaurants and shops I wanted to explore, and I enjoyed the space I created. I sat in a cozy café, reading a book about energy therapy. I took notes and journaled my own experiences. I was completely content being on my own, and it felt amazing.

After I left, I kept driving and found new little discoveries along the way, embracing my emotions as they came up and enjoying my own company. I couldn't recall ever being so content in my own skin as I had on that adventure. I felt brave, confident, and ready to spend even more time with myself. I had a feeling I was going to like what I discovered.

And I have. I now know I'm due for a date day when I'm tired and edgy for several days, and I don't want to do anything for anyone else but force myself to anyway, which, of course, creates resentment and natural angst. These are my symptoms of disconnection from myself and clues that I am proportionally giving more than I am receiving. It's my cue that it's time for me to prioritize my own needs if I want to feel good about giving and not feel frustrated.

I have been on countless date days with myself since then, and I have to say, each time I enjoy my own company even more; away from expectations, away from responsibility. I always come home feeling refreshed and reconnected to myself. Every. Single. Time.

Now it's your turn.

If you could do whatever you wanted for a day, what would you do? If you start to feel like you can't take the time to be alone, then ask yourself why you are any less important than anyone or anything else you'd take the day for without even questioning it.

Plan a Date Day

If you could plan a day or even an hour for yourself, what would you do? It's time to plan it out. Any amount of time you can fully commit to yourself and do something that you really enjoy with you and you alone is perfect. Ideally, this day or hour will be planned within the next couple of weeks.

What feels relaxing and luxurious? What feels inspiring and exciting? What makes your heart sing? Commit to doing at least one or two of these activities on your own. Create a plan of what you will do on your date.

_____

_____

_____

_____

_____

_____

_____

_____

_____

_____

_____

_____

_____

_____

_____

_____

_____

_____

_____

_____

_____

_____

_____

_____

_____

Today's Reflection:

What brought you joy, whether intentional or unexpected? What was meaningful and special about today? Did you live in the flow or resist? How did you live serendipitously? _____

_____

_____

_____

_____

_____

_____

_____

Day 28

A body is a body, but only voices are capable of love.

—Ricardo Piglia

You know all those voices in your head? The ones that feel like they are nonstop talking to each other? They are perfectly normal. We all have them. They come with different tones, words, and motives, each playing a distinct role in our decision-making thought process and behavior.

These voices or parts of ourselves play a vital role in the way we judge, often condemning the voices we feel as negative or hurtful, yet rarely empowering the voices which are positive and uplifting.

You may have said, "Part of me feels this way and the other part feels that way." You might describe them as the angel and devil on your shoulders, dueling it out. Or maybe you relate the voices to people you know who have impacted you. Regardless of how you label them, they are part of your makeup and you direct the role in the play they are starring in.

When this activity developed, I had already completed my *30 Days to Me*. It came after I listened to my clients go to war with themselves. It dawned on me that most of our challenges come from the barrage of opinions and feisty triggers that get us arguing with ourselves and being downright mean.

I had some resistance with this activity. Even though I had many voices in my head, I wasn't sure I wanted to list them all out! My own fear of teaching them each to get along came from knowing this was a key way to changing my behavior, and that meant taking ownership, and that meant being responsible and not blaming anyone or anything else for my hardships. And where's the fun in that?

I jest, but really, I get it. I've spent a lot of time blaming others for how I feel. It wasn't until I actually owned the fact that it was my own insecurities interacting with the outside world that I actually began to feel more in control of myself. And the more I understand and accept them, the more I have been willing and able to change my responses.

What I found most interesting was recognizing that the conversations I had to pay the most attention to and support were the ones inside me, at this twenty-four-hour dinner party I was hosting. I'm well trained in listening to others and reframing their conversations, but I was less impressive in listening to my own and helping them out. With a little self-awareness and a whole lot of practice in compassion, I am becoming a fine hostess for myself and my lovely chatty parts. I would totally hang out with us.

With that said, I do not find this easy. However, I do find it helpful. When I speak to my angry, hurt, and anxious parts with more respect and kindness, I find it creates a more immediate sense of calm than when I ignore them or try to distract them. It is not automatic for me. I have to consciously step back and listen. I find this very uncomfortable at times because I am impatient with my discomfort and I want immediate results. I believe the peace is worth the effort and because of this I will keep practicing—and then practice some more.

Now it's your turn.

Identifying your various voices allows you a glimpse into who you are and how you process. It helps you to see that although you have many views, the goal is to get them to compromise and support each other, instead of ignoring or pushing each other around or out. The more you can respect each and every part of yourself, the more you have an understanding of yourself. The more compassion you feel, the less negative judgment you feel for yourself as well as others.

Remember: everyone has many parts of themselves.

Parts of Self Question

We all have parts of ourselves that interact and work with each other. These same parts can also work vehemently against each other at times. Yet each part plays a valuable role in our lives and as our authentic selves.

Imagine you are having a dinner party with the different parts of you. Each has a seat at the table. As the host of the party, you must introduce the parts of yourself. Give them names and brief descriptions of what they add to your life or what they take away. Who is invited first to the party? Who is likely asked to leave first? Who are the dominant players? Who do you wish would make a stronger appearance? What needs to be adjusted to allow your different parts to work together?

If you're hosting a dinner party, the idea is to give everyone a chance to be heard. It's good manners, really. Everyone in the room of our minds has a voice, and they each play a significant role in our whole and authentic selves. To wish them away or quiet them is to tell them they have no use, and that is simply not true. Our fears have protected us just as many times as our sense of rationalization has calmed us. They are all worthy of our attention.

_____

_____

_____

_____

_____

_____

Today's Reflection:

What brought you joy, whether intentional or unexpected? What was meaningful and special about today? Did you live in the flow or resist? How did you live serendipitously? _____

_____

_____

_____

_____

_____

_____

Day 29

I remind myself every morning: Nothing I say this day will teach me anything. So if I'm going to learn, I must do it by listening.

—*Larry King*

Life is full of chatter and noise, and it can be very difficult to truly listen at times. How do you know when someone is really listening to you? How does it feel? How often do you listen to yourself? Can you cut out the noise and genuinely hear what is being said?

When you listen to people speak, are you waiting to share your views and decide how you're going to respond, or are you hearing what is being said?

Listening is not automatic; it is a practiced skill. It requires intention as well as attention.

My career is based on my ability to listen well. With that said, I can easily space out and drift off, because my attention span is of normal human capacity. I rely not only on what I hear, but also on the way I feel when I am listening to someone.

If I feel edgy, it's usually because I'm feeling their anxiety or angst. Yet it can also be my own impatience if I feel I'm listening to a script on repeat. I'm human, and even old scripts on repeat are frustrating to a professional listener, especially because I know I have several myself. I believe we call them "excuses."

If I feel excitement, it's often because I feel their own, but sometimes it's because I feel a big breakthrough coming that may be just of out their view, and I'm excited by the prospect for them.

I like to feel their emotions, because it gives me a good indication of how they are feeling about whatever they are talking about, and that allows me the opportunity to validate their experience. It also gives me an indication of how I am feeling about it, so I can be aware not to transfer any biases or judgments.

One of the most important practices I use as a listener is to listen for what is not being said; the emotions/fears/dreams that are underneath the words people use. This is where the truth lies, and the more I practice attentively listening, the more I understand other people and myself.

This is also helpful when I'm listening to myself talk to others. I can feel my apprehension if I begin to feel vulnerable or have fears of judgment. I can also hear my voice go up and get fast when I'm talking about something I feel passionate about, literally raising my vibration. This gives me a sense of what is going on with me, what I am avoiding or where I want to put my focus. Practicing listening to others helps me listen to myself.

Now it's your turn.

Do you ever notice that you give the best advice to others and question why you are not taking it yourself?

Why? Because you are like the rest of us. We are naturally egocentric beings who compare everything people say to our experiences and viewpoints. When you listen to others, you learn about yourself. The more you intently listen and take in, the more you learn. As your understanding of yourself increases, it becomes easier to engage your natural compassion to support other people, as well as yourself. It's a circular pattern worth following.

This practice is so important when you are connecting with yourself. In order to hear your inner voice of guidance, it becomes vital that you learn to sit in silence to listen. This is where the stillness practice comes in handy.

Learning to be still helps you to cut through some of your busy thoughts. We are masters of distraction, and although we often hear ourselves say we want peace, we rarely give ourselves the opportunity to feel it. Taking time to ask why gives you invaluable information about yourself.

Listening Question

Practice listening to what is being said to you today and what is not being said. Notice how you feel when you are truly listening and ingesting the words that people say. In addition, practice listening to yourself. How do you feel when you hear your own words? Are you listening and speaking from your heart? How do you know?

Remember: listening is a practice and requires intention, as well as attention.

Think how good it feels when you know you are being heard. Wouldn't it be nice to feel that all the time?

Today seems like a fine time to start.

Write down your observations when you intentionally listened to yourself or someone else today.

_____

_____

_____

_____

_____

_____

_____

_____

Today's Reflection:

What brought you joy, whether intentional or unexpected? What was meaningful and special about today? Did you live in the flow or resist? How did you live serendipitously? _____

_____

_____

_____

_____

_____

_____

_____

Day 30

We love life, not because we are used to living but because we are used to loving.

—Friedrich Nietzsche

The end of life is not something we tend to want to focus on. We spend our time finding ways to live or seeing what is blocking us from spending our days doing exactly what we want. Many of us fear death because we see it as the ending we are trying to avoid.

Yet what if death is not the end? What if it's meant to remind us that this life of ours is short enough to cherish it, but long enough to make our dreams come true? What if it's just a benchmark for progress for our soul and what it wants to accomplish?

What if death is an exit plan to the next realm, where all we leave behind are the lessons we learned and gifts we gave to those we came in contact with? What if it's our end goal of a life well lived in this season before we transition and move onto the next?

When I wrote my own eulogy, I was on my last day of the *30 Days to Me*, vacationing at my family's lake compound in the woods of Maine.

Several people who had major impacts on my life had lived and died there, my mother included. It seemed a fitting place to write my own eulogy of how I wanted to end this part of my existence, in this body, in this life.

I wrote my end goal. I wrote how I wanted to see myself and how I wanted to be seen. I wrote what I wanted to feel and what I truly found valuable. I wrote about my accomplishments and what inspired me. And what I found was that I inspire me. I was craving to continue this transformation to be the best version of myself, and I would not stop continuing to mold her.

I've been given this modeling clay, and I am the only one responsible for sculpting it. People can influence me, but I am the masterpiece of my own life—me and me alone.

I came into this world with one piece of clay, and I will leave it with the same. How will I choose to mold it? That is what I choose each day.

Now it's your turn.

What is the legacy you want to leave behind? What do you want people to learn from you? How do you want to be known in your absence?

This is your script. Write it as you wish.

What will the masterpiece of your life look like?

Eulogy Question

Life is an unlimited opportunity to create dreams and fulfill them, to touch hearts and make them come alive, and to capture the beauty in every experience we are offered.

When we die, we are left with a dash between the day we are born and the day we leave this world. What do you want your dash to be? What legacy do you want to create? How do you want to be remembered? How do you want to live? How do you want to love?

Write your own eulogy, putting life in perspective of who you want to be and what you want to leave behind. Focus on the ways you celebrate life.

_____

_____

Today's Reflection:

What brought you joy, whether intentional or unexpected? What was meaningful and special about today? Did you live in the flow or resist? How did you live serendipitously? _____

_____

_____

_____

_____

_____

_____

_____

Congratulations!

You Made It! On day thirty-one, do something special to celebrate and honor yourself, by being your most authentic self. Speak to yourself and others with kindness. Make decisions that feel right to you. Spend time with people who make your heart sing. Feel gratitude for all the good in your life. Honor the moments that aren't perfect, and praise the ones that are. Be you and love you. And be proud. Being you is the bravest and strongest way to live. You're doing it. Happy *30 Days to You!*

About the Author

Lynn Reilly is an Author, Licensed Professional Counselor and a Master Energy Therapist whose passion is educating people how to understand and support themselves while living a Serendipitous life…a life filled with unexpected joy and passion…a life meant to be.

Her innate skill of seeing and feeling thought and behavior patterns shaped her to become an expert in understanding the how's and why's of human behavior. However, her ability to see the beauty and unexpected gifts which rise from all of our experiences is what she enjoys sharing the most. Since life's best education comes from experience over theory, Lynn has been given countless opportunities to experience incredibly painful situations and circumstances and discover ways to grow through them and use them to her advantage. Her work is designed to support and inspire others to do the same.

Learn more about Lynn at livingwithserendipity.com